LITTLE ARTHUR'S

HISTORY OF ENGLAND

The Century Edition

Their Majesties King George the Sixth and his Consort, Queen Elizabeth, with their Daughters. Coronation Day, 1937.

LITTLE ARTHUR'S
HISTORY OF ENGLAND

BY MARIA, LADY CALLCOTT

THE CENTURY EDITION

WITH A MEMOIR ADDED
AND ILLUSTRATIONS

REVISED
TO BRING THE HISTORY TO THE CORONATION OF
HIS MAJESTY KING GEORGE THE SIXTH

LONDON
JOHN MURRAY, ALBEMARLE STREET, W.

First Edition	.	. .	*August,* 1835
Century Edition	.	.	*March,* 1936
Revised		. .	*May,* 1937
Reprinted		. . .	*January,* 1941

CONTENTS

CONTENTS

LIST OF ILLUSTRATIONS

LADY CALLCOTT.

From the oil painting by Sir Thomas Lawrence, P.R.A.,
in the National Portrait Gallery.

LADY CALLCOTT AND HER BOOK

The fact that "Little Arthur's History of England" has healthily outlived a hundred years is one which those who knew and enjoyed the book in childhood will understand better than those who come to it for the first time now and are necessarily without the illusions—on books and other things—which, looked back upon, were a sustaining part of the more arduous and disciplined childhood of, let us say, the serious 'seventies.

I remember the shock I had when, in 1880, I discovered that my own treasured copy had been given to the local hospital with the compliments of the dishonest donor ; as well as the consolatory thrill that came when, seventeen years afterwards, having found my way to Mr. Murray's at Albemarle Street, I rediscovered the book and renewed acquaintance with its illustrations, especially that of the murder of Edward, King and Martyr, at the instigation of his wicked stepmother Elfrida—not only for the dramatic, cold-blooded cruelty of the incident depicted, which had its charm for simple childhood—but also because I found myself intrigued as to where Edward's back really began as judged by the direction of the murderer's knife ; which, in spite of the statement in the text, seems to be threatening the royal person elsewhere.

Be that so or not, this delightful work has well earned its century and is so far from being " out " that here it is celebrating the event with a reset and considerately revised edition, that also marks the Accession to the Throne of King Edward the Eighth and, incidentally, the 150th anniversary of its author's birth.

It was first published in August, 1835, in two octodecimo volumes, and was to have had on the cover a representation of Little Arthur himself, but want of time, it appears, prevented that, and therefore we cannot know what the ever-attentive child looked like. There were six " embellishments in wood " in the text, with the attractive design that is still on the title-page ; crown, sceptre, sword and scales of justice and scroll of the Great Charter resting on—can it be the block ? If that be so then, sinister as it may seem, it was a symbol appropriate to the book that, while it detailed the rights and privileges of Englishmen, did not fail also to urge the truth that the abuse of those rights and privileges ended for many with the sharp arbitrament of the axe.

The purpose of those early woodcuts was to illustrate the occasions when children were the heroes of the stories told and, therefore, Little Arthur was shown pictures of Alfred at his mother's knee, of his namesake with Hubert de Burgh, of the Princes in the Tower, of the two young children of Charles the First saying farewell to their father and, passing into the 'teens, of Lady Jane Grey refusing the crown. The other woodcut finds the expected children transformed into an episode of the Battle of Hastings. In later editions all those illustrations—with many others added—were redrawn to their improvement, with the exception of the vigorous glimpse of 1066, which remains as it was.

The author's name was given in advertisements and at the end of the Preface, " To Mothers," as " M. C—— " ; with the consequence that the many bright people who will sometimes go wrong ascribed the book for a time to Miss Croker.

The first edition was so successful that seven hundred copies were promptly sold. A second edition in one volume was published in 1837, and in the following year two more impressions were called for ; and so it has gone on continuously ever since, with the result that seventy editions, comprising some 800,000 copies, have been issued and sold in the hundred years.

But it is time to pay tribute to Lady Callcott, who not only wrote a living and fascinating history for intelligent children, but expressed through its pages an attractive personality which her letters confirm.

Maria Dundas, the daughter of a rear-admiral, was born near Cockermouth in 1785. As her father was for some years on duty abroad, she spent her holidays with her uncle Sir David Dundas. He was cultured, and fortunate in possessing many friends of high mind and good taste whose influence, doubtless, was stimulating and inspiring to his impressionable young niece and probably led her to take up literature as her profession. Among those friends were the poets Rogers and Campbell, and the young artist, Thomas Lawrence, whose unfinished portrait of her, painted when they met at Rome some years afterwards, hangs in the National Portrait Gallery and is reproduced on p. xii. When she was twenty-three Maria went with her father to India, and so began her far travels over the Earth, visiting Asia, Europe and South America, and storing her mind with impressions and information which were to prove valuable to others, as well as to herself, when she came to write and to give advice to other aspirants in literature. In all ways her life in its earlier years comprised an excellent apprenticeship to her subsequent trade of letters.

On the way to India she met, and in Bombay married, Captain Thomas Graham of the Royal Navy. He seems to have been a genial, kindly man and typical British sailor. Two years later they came home ; he to resume his career in the Navy until he went on half-pay, when they were compelled to practise the simple life with severe economy, and she to become deeply immersed in literature, as an author, and later as a reader of manuscripts for the second John Murray.

Her meeting with the publisher was important for her, as not only did she gain thereby the stimulus—the practical and intellectual stimulus, as it may be called in her case—which came through his masterly association with " the traffic of mind and literature," as she termed it in a letter to him, but he introduced her to authors and others whose friendly and brilliant sociabilities were to make the drawing-room of his new home in Albemarle Street famous. Beside the intellectual and practical gains to her from that association, she also was brought into his family-circle and became the godmother of one of his daughters, who was named after her, Maria.

For a time she lived in Scotland—in Perthshire and at Broughty Ferry in Angus—and was so lonely there, " in this poor, proud country, where Montrose and Dundee are still in the mouths of the very people," with Graham, as she called her husband, only sometimes ashore, that the flights of the red cross-bills from Russia and the passing of the ships were notable events of the day. She does, however, record one heroic occasion which improved that standstill time. Whales came into the harbour at Broughty Ferry and there was a fight in the shallow between a currier with his knife and a finner. The currier having plunged his blade into the whale was knocked head over heels into the water ; whereupon a sailor leapt on the creature and swam Arion-like round the harbour, holding by the back fin. The poor thing died.

John Murray helped in the monotony of her very retired

life there by keeping her supplied with books, and, in a wide selection which included many works of travel, she seems to have enjoyed best " Emma," the Sagas of Iceland, Byron's younger efforts—it was before he went into exile and discovered the genius of " Don Juan "—and the " Christabel " of Coleridge, being thrilled by its eeriness—"those shrunken serpent's eyes." Naturally, in the circumstances, she tried her own gifts for verse ; but judged by the examples preserved at Albemarle Street her efforts were conventional, sapless, and at best reminiscent of Lord Byron not far from his worst. For that poet, the "Pilgrim of Eternity," in those his golden years, she had an admiration somewhat more than sweetly reasonable ; and even later, when the world and the flesh, his follies and misfortunes, had blurred his fineness of mind and spirit, she still regarded him with the pity of admiration, as one might a lamed and banished god.

In 1821 Graham was appointed to the command of H.M.S. " Doris " and with protracted delays on the way sailed with his wife to South America, reaching Pernambuco just at the outbreak of civil war in Brazil. The voyage was continued and, as usual in those years and seas, was long and boisterous. On that occasion, alas, it also was tragical, for when they were off Cape Horn Captain Graham died.

His widow, after some time spent in South America, came home and then returned to Brazil where she became the instructress to the little princess (who bargained that the lessons shouldn't be long), a daughter of Don Pedro, the new, but, as it proved, transient Emperor of that country. During her stay there she met again the brilliant Lord Cochrane, at that time in command of the Brazilian Navy, and became his eager champion then and afterwards against the misunderstandings of those who obstinately doubted and opposed him.

Four years afterwards she married Augustus W. Callcott, R.A., who later was knighted, and again the union was happy. But in November 1842, after eleven years of increasing weakness and illness, following the breaking of a blood-vessel, she died. That is the simple life-story of a woman of talent, devoted industry and charm, whose powers of sympathy and friendship were jewels.

Lady Callcott was sincere, she had her likes and dislikes and she enjoyed telling a story ; and that is why " Little Arthur " is still so very readable a book. She saw the romance that is an actual part of history, as real as and more effective anyhow than the sand and statistics that some others have made of it ; and recognised not only that the Edwards and Richards and Williams who sat on the British throne were picturesque figures in their robes or armour, but also that through their personalities they were positive influences, definitely good or, with rare exceptions, utterly bad, on the government and fortunes of their country. She did not mince her judgments. She had something of the faculty that certain greater historians than she have possessed of seeing the characters in the pageantry of history in such vividly revealing lights that the shadows cast by them were, therefore, the darker ; and most of her leading actors were either " clever " and " handsome " or " wicked " and " cruel " ; while in her earlier pages she was apt to overwork the helpful but hazardous " very."

Naturally, her history, written a hundred years ago, has needed adjustments as research and discoveries have modified the values of many old-accepted events and has required from time to time some shadowy and anonymous continuer (to borrow the expression of a witty lady writing in the "Spectator ") to mend the incidental mistakes and misjudgments and carry on the narrative. The first revision was done, in 1879, by Mr. James Rowley, a serious historian, as we can justly call him, knowing little else about him, who went through the book and while correcting errors added a few sanctimonious touches here and there, going so far as to take out Lady Callcott's fine moral of Alfred, at the end of Chapter nine, and substituting for it a sort of sermonic tag. As Mr. Rowley, in a letter to the third John Murray, confessed that his amendment was conjectural while hers, he had a " suspicion," was based upon a spurious thirteenth-century work entitled " The Proverbs of Alfred," I have replaced that as, after all, this is Lady Callcott's book and unless she was provedly wrong her own words should be preferred to his or to anyone else's. " It is some comfort," said Rowley, " to be able to speculate that errors of Lady Callcott's kind will be more easily shaken off by the Little Arthurs of the present day when they come to know more, than errors of the opposite school that is not so aggressive." True and comforting—but oh, those opposite and aggressive schools, whatever they were ! What mischief have they wrought to the honest domain of History !

In my revision I have been scrupulously careful to keep to the spirit and, so far as might be, the phrasing of Lady Callcott's work and have made only such modifications as later discoveries or the better interpretation of incidents have justified. Richard the Third, for instance, was not quite the ultra-melodramatic villain that she and Shakespeare made of him ; but all that I have done, because of the uncertainties abounding even in his case, is to remind Little Arthur that the stories told of that King were possibly in large measure untrue ; for his bitter enemies after the seventh Henry had come to the throne had nobody with authority or courage enough to gainsay their wild assertions (and we know even in milder times what political misrepresentations may be). Also, I have removed from before the name of Mary Tudor the opprobrious adjective that reddened it too darkly ; for the reasons that, with all her bigotry and the cruelties countenanced and done by her, she was a most unhappy woman who had been sorely mistreated ; she did try to save —and saved—some of the persecuted of those cruel times, and, on the whole, was as much to be pitied as blamed. The word, moreover, was one that never was or could be suited to the ears and the lips of children.

As to the rest, the book remains an admirable history for those to whom it was addressed. It arouses a right interest in the story of the growth in power, responsibility and honourable glory of our race ; while also it inspires the essential ideals of patriotism, unselfishness and duty.

C. E. LAWRENCE

Accession Day, 1936.

PREFACE TO THE FIRST EDITION
TO MOTHERS

Though I have not the happiness to be a mother, my love of Children has led me to think a good deal about them, their amusements, and their lessons.

This little HISTORY was written for a real little ARTHUR, and I have endeavoured to *write* it nearly as I would *tell* it to an intelligent child. I well remember what I wanted to be told myself, in addition to what I found in my lesson book, when I was first allowed to read the History of England, and I hope I have answered most of the questions I recollect to have wished to ask.

I may have failed in satisfying the almost boundless inquiries of intelligent children, and I could wish that the mother or governess who may put this little book into the hand of her pupils, would read each chapter herself before she gives it to a child, that she may be ready with answers to such questions as the chapter may suggest.

Perhaps I have not made my small volume amusing enough to answer the purpose of those who wish children to learn everything in play. I do not know that I could have done so if I wished it : there are some things to be learned from the History of England, that are of some import to the future life of a child, and are no play : things, independent of the change of kings, or the fighting of battles, or even of the pathetic tales in which every true history is rich.

These things I have tried to teach in a way to engage the attention, and to fix them in the memory, till advancing age, and the reading of history in detail, shall call them into use.

Next to the study of the Sacred Scriptures, I have always held the history of our own country to be important in education, particularly in that of boys.

To teach the love of our country is almost a religious duty. In the Scriptures how often is it referred to? How many beautiful passages in the Psalms encourage it? "If I forget thee, O Jerusalem, let my right hand forget her cunning." But above all other tender expressions, is that of the blessed Jesus, addressed to Jerusalem and its inhabitants: "How often would I have gathered thy children together, as a hen doth gather her brood under her wings, and ye would not!"

Let no one fear, that to cultivate patriotism, is to make men illiberal in feeling towards mankind in general. Is any man the worse citizen for being a good son, or brother, or father, or husband?

I am indeed persuaded that the well-grounded love of our own country, is the best security for that enlightened philanthropy which is aimed at as the perfection of moral education.

This is the feeling that has guided me in writing "LITTLE ARTHUR'S HISTORY." If it should happily lay the foundation for patriotism in one single Englishman, my wishes will be answered, my best hopes fulfilled.

M. C.

CHAPTER I

THE ANCIENT BRITONS

You know, my dear little Arthur, that the country you live in is called ENGLAND. It is joined to another country called SCOTLAND, and the two together with WALES are called GREAT BRITAIN.

Now, a very long time ago, Britain was so full of trees, that there was very little room for houses, and still less for corn-fields, and there were no gardens.

The houses were made of wicker-work ; that is, of sticks put together like baskets, and plastered over with mud, to keep out the wind and rain ; and the people, who were called Britons, used to build a good many together, and make a fence round them, to keep the bears, and the wolves, and the foxes, which lived in their woods, from coming in the night to steal their sheep, or perhaps to kill their children, while they were asleep.

These fences were made of great piles of wood and trunks of trees, laid one upon another till they were as high as a wall ; for at that time the Britons did not know how to build walls of stone or of bricks with mortar.

Several houses, with a fence round them, made a town ; and the Britons had their towns either in the middle of the woods, where they could hardly be found out, or else on the tops of high hills, from which they could see everything and everybody that was coming near them.

I do not think the insides of their houses could have been

very comfortable. They had possibly wooden stools to sit on, and wooden benches for bedsteads, and their beds were made of skins of wild beasts, spread over dry grass and leaves. In some places they used the pretty heath that grows upon the commons for beds, and, in others, nothing but dry leaves spread upon the ground. They had great wooden bowls to hold their meat, and wooden cups to drink out of ; and in some parts of the country they had coarse earthen bowls and pitchers, some of which you may now see in many museums.

They had very few tools to make the things they wanted ; and yet, by taking great pains, they made them very neatly. Their boats were very curious ; they were nicely made, of basket-work covered over with leather ; they were called coracles.

You may think that, as the Britons had such poor houses and beds, they were not much better off for clothes.

In the winter they used to wrap themselves up in the skins of the beasts they could shoot with their bows and arrows. In the summer they were naked, and instead of clothes they put paint upon their bodies. They were very fond of a fine blue colour, made out of a plant, called Woad, which they found in their woods. They squeezed out the juice of the Woad, and then stained themselves all over with it, so that in summer they looked as if they were dressed in tight blue clothes.

They were as ill off for eating as for clothes. Only a few of the very richest Britons could get bread, the rest of the people ate acorns and berries, which they found in the woods, instead of bread. They had beef, mutton, and deer, and hares, and wild birds. They drank milk, and knew how to make cheese ; but most of them were forced to spend a good deal of time in hunting for wild animals in the woods, and often went without their dinners when they could not get near enough to a beast or bird to shoot it with their arrows.

In time, however, the Britons in the south learned how to grow corn, to work in metal, and other useful things. They traded with the nearest part of Europe, which is now called France, but was then named Gaul. They were very brave in war, and fought on foot and from chariots, which had sharp blades like scythes sticking out to cut down the enemies as they were driven through their ranks.

CHAPTER II

THE DRUIDS

I am sorry to say that the old Britons had no churches ; and they did not know anything about the true God. Their oldest and cleverest men only thought God must be somewhere, and because they saw that oaks were the largest, and oldest, and best trees in the woods, they told the people that God must be where the oaks grew ; but they were mistaken, you know, for God is in heaven, and He made the oaks, and everything else that you can see, and everything that you can think of. But as these poor people did not know any better, they chose some of the oldest and wisest men to be their priests, and to say prayers for them, under the shade of the oaks. These priests they called DRUIDS. They had long white beards, and wore better clothes than the other people, for they had white linen robes. They knew how to cure sick people, by giving them different parts of the plants that grew in the woods ; and if they were burnt, or cut, they made salves to heal them ; and they would not teach the common people how to use these things of themselves, so everybody was obliged to go to them for help. And the people gave the Druids a part of what they had, whether it was corn, or warm skins to make beds of, or paint, or tin, or copper, or silver, that they found among the mountains, for curing them.

One of the things they used to cure the sick people with was a plant called mistletoe. It does not grow on the ground, but on the branches of trees ; sometimes, but rarely, on the oak. The Druids knew the time of year when its berries were ripe, and made a great feast, and all the people came to it ; and the oldest Druid, dressed in white, and with a white band round his head, used to take a golden sickle, and go up into the trees where the mistletoe grew and cut it while the others sang songs, and said some prayers to their false gods, because they did not know the true God.

These Druids used to advise the kings what to do, and what rules to give the people ; and because nobody in England could write, the Druids made songs and verses about everything that happened, and taught them to the young people, that they might teach them again to their children. Those who made these songs were called BARDS.

Now you know that, though it is a very good thing to be able to repeat fine verses about things that happened long ago, it is much better to have them written down ; because people might forget some of the verses, and then their children would not know what had happened in their country before they lived themselves.

And so it was with the Druids. People began to forget the oldest verses, when something happened that I will tell you about in the next chapter, by means of which the Britons learned not only to write and read, but to know the true God.

CHAPTER III

THE ROMAN CONQUEST

There is a city called ROME, a good way from England, and the people belonging to it are called ROMANS.

Now, at the time I told you of, when the poor Britons were so ill off for almost everything, the Romans were the cleverest and bravest people in the world. By their bravery they had conquered all the countries between Rome and England, which you know was then called Britain ; and by being able to write better than any other people at that time, they made books, in which they set down everything that happened to them and to the people they conquered.

One of their wisest and greatest men, called JULIUS CÆSAR, wrote what I have told you about Britain, and some more that I am going to tell you. When the Romans had found out that there was such a country as Britain, some sailors and merchants came here to see what the country and the people were like.

And they saw that the people were strong and well made, and found that they were intelligent, and good tempered, and they wished to have some of them for servants, and some for soldiers. And they saw too that the country was very pretty, and that if anybody who knew how to build nice houses, and to make proper fields, were to live here, it would be a very pleasant place indeed.

Besides all this, they found that some of the best tin and copper in the world was found in one part of England, and sometimes the people found gold and silver too. Then they saw among the shells by the sea-side, and in some of the rivers, some of those beautiful round white things called pearls, which ladies have always been fond of stringing and making necklaces of.

So when they went home to Rome, they told everybody of all the good things they had seen in Britain ; and the great men in Rome determined to go and conquer the whole country, that they might make servants of the people, and take their land, and make corn-fields for themselves, and get all the tin, and copper, and silver, and gold, and pearls, and take them to Rome.

The Romans had sent some very brave soldiers, with their great captain, the same Julius Cæsar who wrote down these things, to conquer Gaul ; and they crossed the sea in order to conquer Britain ; but they did not find it so easy to do as they had hoped it would be. Although the poor Britons were almost naked, and had very bad swords, and poor spears and bows and arrows, and small shields, made of basket-work covered with leather, they were so brave, that they fought a great many battles against the Romans, who had everything they could want to fight with, before they would give up any part of their country to them.

At last, when the Romans had gotten a part of Britain, they were obliged to build strong walls all about their houses. And their houses and walls were made of good stone and brick, instead of the trunks and branches of trees, such as the Britons used. And the Roman soldiers were obliged to keep watch always, because the Britons were trying every day to drive them away ; and they kept good swords and spears, and great shields, covered with plates of iron ; and they put pieces of iron on their backs and their breasts, and their arms and legs, and called it armour, so the bad swords of the Briton could hardly ever hurt a Roman ; but their bows and arrows, which they managed very well, killed a good many.

However, the Romans remained masters at last, and they made the Britons cut down many of their woods, and turn the ground into corn-fields and gardens for them ; and forced them to dig the tin and copper out of the earth for them, and to fish in the seas and rivers, to find pearls for the Roman ladies ; and the poor Britons were very unhappy, because they had lost their freedom, and could never do as they liked.

But I must end this chapter. In the next I will tell you how God turned the unhappiness of the Britons into much that was very good for them.

CHAPTER IV

INFLUENCE OF THE ROMANS

You remember, I hope, what you read in the first chapter, about the uncomfortable houses of the Britons, how badly they were dressed, and how often they were obliged to be hungry when they could not catch the birds or beasts in the woods.

Now when God allowed the Romans to come and take part of the country of the Britons, and to make servants of the people, He put it into the hearts of the Romans to teach the Britons most of the things they knew themselves, and the Romans who came to Britain wrote books, from which we learn the way in which these things were done.

By employing the Britons to help them to build their houses and walls of stone or brick, they taught them how to make good ones for themselves ; then by making them learn to spin and weave the wool that grew upon their sheep, they gave them means to make better clothes, both for winter and summer, than they had thought of before ; and they left off staining their skins with the juice of plants, and began to wash themselves, and to keep their hair neat, and even to put on ornaments like the Romans.

When they saw how the Romans ploughed the fields, and made enough corn grow to make bread for everybody, as well as for the rich people, they began to do the same ; and they began to like to have gardens for cabbages and onions, and apples and roses, all four of which the Romans taught

9

them to plant, besides some other useful things which I have forgotten.

But, what was much better than all the rest, the Romans built schools, and had school-masters to teach their children to read and write, and the little Britons were allowed to go to these schools as well as the little Romans ; and, as the Britons were very intelligent, you may think how soon they learned to read and write, and how glad their fathers and mothers were to find them so improved.

You see, therefore, that when God allowed the Romans to conquer the Britons, He made them the means of teaching them a great many useful things ; above all, how to read.

Many years after the Romans first took the country for themselves there came some good men, who brought the Bible with them, and began to teach both the Romans and the Britons, who could read, all about the true God, and how they ought to serve Him, and love Him. And they told them to love one another, instead of fighting. And by degrees they made the Britons forget the Druids, and leave off praying under the oaks. And they built several churches, and a great many Britons became Christians, and learned to thank God for sending the Romans to their country to teach them to be wiser and better, and happier than they were before.

You may suppose that all these things took a good deal of time to do ; indeed, they took a great many years, and in that time there were many different Roman governors. And when you are a little older, and know more about England, you will read something about them in the large History of England, and in some other books.

CHAPTER V

LONDON AND OTHER TOWNS

I told you what poor and small places the British towns were, before the Romans came here. They soon taught the Britons to make them better. London was one of their towns ; it was so hid among trees that it could hardly be seen ; but the Romans soon cut down a good many of the trees round it, and built large houses there to live in. And they made a market, which you know is a place where people go to sell the things they had provided and to buy other things. At first they only changed one thing for another ; I mean, that if one man wanted a pair of shoes, he went to the shoemaker, and said, Give me a pair of shoes and I will give you a shirt, or some chickens, or something that I have and do not want myself, if you will give me the shoes. But this was trouble-some, because people could not easily carry enough things about to make exchanges with. So, when the Romans came, they began to use money to buy the things they wanted, and the money was made of the silver and copper found in England.

Well, besides the good houses and the market the Romans made in London, they built a wall round it, made of stone and brick mixed, and a tower. Now a tower is a high and strong building ; and it was used long ago to put money and other things into, to keep them safe. And if any enemies came to fight the people of the country, they used to put the women and children into their towers, while the strong men went to fight their enemies, and drive them away. Towers have not these uses nowadays, when we enjoy peace and safety in our open houses and the soldiers and police protect us ; while towers and castles fall into ruin and then are looked at as curiosities. Another sort of tower, you know, is built by the side, or at the end, of a church, to hang the bells in, that people may know it is time to go to prayers, when they hear the bells ring.

Though the Romans took so much pains with London, they did not forget the other towns of the Britons, but made them all much better. I will tell you the names of some they did most good to. First, there was Bath, where the Britons showed them some springs of warm water, which were used to cure sick people. Drinking the water was good for some, and bathing in it for others. Now, Bath was a very pretty place, and the Romans made it prettier, by building beautiful houses to bathe in, and making fine gardens to their own houses ; and many of the great men, and some Roman ladies, loved to live there. And the Britons followed their example, and began to have fine houses, and to plant beautiful gardens, and some of them went to Rome to learn more than they could learn in Britain ; and, when they came back, they taught others what they had learned.

Then there was York, the largest town next to London of those that the Romans took the trouble to make much better than the old Britons had done.

Besides houses, and towers, and walls, the Romans built some good schools in York, and I have even heard that there was a *library* in York, in the time of the Romans ; but I am not quite sure of this.

But I should never finish my chapter, and you would be very tired, if I were to try to tell you every one of the names of the British towns that the Romans improved ; in all, I dare say, they are more than a hundred.

They also made good roads throughout the country, some of which remain in use to this day.

CHAPTER VI

THE ANGLES AND SAXONS

Everything seemed to be going on well with the Britons and Romans, when a great misfortune happened, which I must tell you about.

Most of the great men in Rome had grown very idle and careless, because they had become so rich and strong that they could do what they pleased, and make everybody else obey them. And they let the soldiers in Rome be idle, instead of keeping them busy about useful things. So they forgot how to fight properly, and when a great many enemies went against Rome, the soldiers there could not drive them away, and they sent, in a hurry, to Britain, for all the good Roman soldiers that were here, as well as the strongest and best Britons, to go and defend them ; so Britain was left without enough men to take care of the towns, and the old men, and the women, and the children.

It happened that very soon after the best Britons had gone away to Rome, a number of people, called ANGLES and SAXONS, came in ships to Britain, and landed. You will remember the Angles, because these were the people who changed the name of half of Britain into Englaland, which we now call England.

At first they took all the gold and silver and clothes and food they could find, and even some of the little children to make servants of, and carried them off in their ships to their own country.

Afterwards the Britons sent to ask their help against some fierce enemies, called the PICTS and SCOTS, who had invaded South Britain from the northern part, which we now call Scotland. So two brothers came over first, who were called HENGIST and HORSA ; Horsa was slain in battle at Aylesford in Kent, but Hengist made himself king over a part of Britain.

And when the other Saxons and Angles saw what good and useful things were to be had in Britain, they determined to go there too. Some of them said they would only rob the Britons, and some said they would try to conquer the whole country, and take it for their own ; and so, after a great deal of fighting, they did. But although a great many of the bravest Britons had been taken to Rome, some of the others joined together, to try and defend their country.

One of the first of them was King Arthur, who was one of the bravest men in the world, and he had some friends who were called his knights. They helped him to fight the Saxons, but the Saxons were too strong for them ; so after fighting a long time, King Arthur was obliged to give up a good deal of his land to them. Yet he beat them at last in a great battle, and was able to keep the rest of his kingdom from them for many years. You will read many pretty stories about King Arthur and his knights, when you are older.

I have heard that they were all so good and so brave that nobody could tell who was the best, and the king himself did not know which to like best, so he had a large round table made, that they might all sit at it, and be equal ; because you know that at a round table the places are all alike, but at a long table one place may seem better than another. But I cannot tell you more about the knights now, for we must think about the Angles and Saxons.

By little and little, the Saxons and Angles drove the natives out of almost all Britain. The greatest number of those who remained went into that part called WALES, where there were high mountains and thick woods, where they could hide themselves. You will read in some books that some went with King Arthur to a part of France, which was called Brittany because Britons were living there already. But we cannot be sure of this.

Now the Angles and Saxons were fierce and cruel, for they had not yet learned anything about the true God ; but instead of loving and serving Him, they made a great many figures of stone and wood, in the shape of men and women, and called them by different names, such as Woden, and Thor, and fancied they could help them and bless them, if they prayed to them ; but you know this was both foolish and wicked. It was foolish, because stones and wood cannot hear or understand ; and wicked, because we ought to pray to the true God only.

The Britons, who had all become Christians before the Angles and Saxons came to Britain, were very ill treated by their new masters, because they would not leave off loving and serving the true God. Their churches were pulled down, and the clergymen either killed or driven away. And the people of England (as Britain now began to be called) were almost in as bad a state as before the Romans came ; for although the Angles and Saxons were glad enough to make them build houses, and plough the corn-fields, and take care of sheep for them, they would not let them read—they spoilt their schools, and burnt the books, besides pulling down the churches, as I told you before.

At length, however, these bad times ended, and the con-querors themselves left off being cruel, and did more good to the country than ever the Romans did, as I will tell you in another chapter.

CHAPTER VII

CONVERSION TO CHRISTIANITY

I told you, in the last chapter, that Hengist made himself king over part of Britain. His kingdom was Kent.

Soon afterwards other brave captains of the Angles and Saxons made themselves kings. So there were seven chief kingdoms in England, besides many petty kings. As soon as they were settled, they and their people began to like the houses and gardens and bathing places the Romans had left in the country, though they destroyed the most of them. But there were few, if any, of the Christian clergymen left among them, to teach them to know the true God. The Angles and Saxons lived as heathens in their new country for more than a hundred years. And now I will tell you how God gave them the word of life, and turned them from their false gods.

Soon after the Anglian and Saxon kings had settled themselves quietly in Britain, a good many boys were taken from Britain to be made servants at Rome. Most of these were Angles, and it happened that as they were standing together an Abbot named GREGORY saw them, and he thought they were very beautiful, and asked where they came from and who they were. He was told they were Angles, from Britain, but that they were not Christians. He was sorry for this, and said if they were Christians they would be *Angels*, not *Angles*.

Now Gregory did not go away and forget this ; but, when he was made Bishop of Rome, he sent for a good man named

17

AUGUSTINE, and asked him if he would go to Britain and
teach these people to be Christians ; and Augustine said he

Gregory and the Angles.

would, and he chose some other good men to help him to
teach them.

When Augustine and his friends got to England they went to ETHELBERT, the king of the part they reached first, and asked leave to teach the people ; and the king gave them leave, and gave them a church in the town of Canterbury, and learned a great deal from them himself. But some of the other kings did not like to be Christians, nor to let their people learn, and were very angry with those who listened to Augustine, and killed some of his friends. But at last, when they saw that the Christians behaved better than those who served the wooden and stone false gods they brought with them from their own country, they allowed their people to learn, and so by degrees they all became Christians.

Ina, who was one of the kings of that part of England which was then called Wessex (but now contains Berkshire, Hampshire, and other counties), was very fond of learning, and old books tell us that he collected a penny from every house where the master could spare it, and sent all these pennies to Rome to pay for a school that he might send the young men to, because they could get better masters in Rome than in England at that time. These pennies were called PETER'S PENCE, and were sent to Rome for a great many years ; but learned men now think that it was not Ina, but a later English king, called Offa, who first began to send them.

Now I must tell you what the young men at that time learned in the school. First of all to read, and to write, and to count ; then to paint pictures in books, and to build beautiful churches, and to plant gardens, and to take care of fruit trees, and to sing well in church. And they taught all these things to their friends when they came back to England.

I should have told you that it was only the clergymen who went to school in Rome ; and when they came home, though some of them lived in houses of their own, yet most went

2*

and lived in large houses, called convents, big enough to hold
a great many of them, besides having schools in them for
teaching children, and rooms where they allowed poor

King Ethelbert declares himself a Christian.

people, who were travelling, to sleep ; and they were good
to the poor and took great care of people who were sick.

And because these clergymen did so much good, the kings
and the people gave them money, and some land fit for corn-
fields and gardens, that they might have plenty for themselves, and the school boys, and the poor.

CHAPTER VIII

THE LAWS OF THE ANGLO-SAXONS

I am sure you wish to hear something more about the Angles and Saxons, now that I have told you that they had become Christians like the Britons, and had left off fighting with them.

There was one thing that they loved above all others, and that was freedom ; that is, they liked that every man should do what he pleased so long as he did not hurt anybody else. And they liked that when a man went into his own house and shut the door he should be safe, and that nobody should go into his house without his leave. Besides that, they liked wicked people to be punished ; but if a man killed another, on purpose, they did not always kill him too ; but they made him give money to the relations of the man he had killed, and perhaps they put him in prison for a while. And the Saxons and Angles liked that when a thief stole anything, he should be made to give it back, and that he should be punished.

Rules like these are called laws, and they are needful, to show men what is wrong and to keep them, if possible, from doing wrong. All laws are meant to do good ; and the Saxons and Angles would not let anybody be punished without taking time to find out what was right.

So chosen men called *Aldermen*, which means the same as *Elder*, were set over different parts of each kingdom to hold courts with the bishop and the lesser nobles, who were called the king's *Thanes* (that is, servants). These courts tried to find out the truth in all disputes, and also before any one was punished for any crime. When the crime was not made out clearly, the man was let off, if he could bring his neighbours to bear witness to his good character. And, in deciding disputes, the judge sometimes took the opinion of twelve men who were told the facts. This was not quite like our trial by jury ; but you see that the people had a share in judging one another.

Sometimes the kings wanted to change their old laws, or to make new ones. But the free people said it was not right or fair to make laws for them without telling them first what they were to be. So when the king wanted to make a new law, he called together his Aldermen and Bishops and Thanes to hear what the new law was to be, and if they liked it they said so, and it was made into a law, and then the people obeyed it, and the judges punished those who did not ; but if they did not like what the king wished, they all said so, and then it was not made into a law. And, besides the Noblemen and Bishops, the people of the towns were called by the king, to hear what the new law was to be.

But it would have been very troublesome for all the men to go to the king every time he wanted to make a new law, or to change an old one, so the men in one town said, It will be better to send three or four of the cleverest of our neighbours to the king, and they can let us know about the new law, and we will tell them what to say for us, and we will stay at home, and plough the fields, and mind our shops and our booths in the market-places ; and so they did ; and the men that were sent by their neighbours went to the king, but they had no share in making the laws.

And when the king, and the nobles and bishops, and the

men who were sent by their neighbours, met all together in one place to talk about the laws, they called it a Witena-gemot, which means, in the old English of those times, a Meeting of the Wise Men. It was something like what we call a Parliament, which means a *talking place*, because they talk about what laws are needed and the best way of making them before they are made.

By these means you see the Angles and Saxons were ruled by laws that they helped to make themselves. And when any of them did wrong, they were not punished till some of their own wise men found out that they really deserved punishment ; and this is what I mean when I tell you that they were a free people who loved freedom.

CHAPTER IX

ALFRED AND THE DANES

You have not forgotten, I hope, that there were seven chief kingdoms of the Angles and Saxons in England. Now, there were many and long wars between these kingdoms ; and also with the Britons who were left in the land. Sometimes one king, and sometimes another, made himself more powerful than all the rest. He was then called *Bretwalda*, which means " Ruler over Britain " ; for the English still called the whole island *Britain*. At last, 827 years after the birth of Christ, the king of *Wessex* (that is, of the West Saxons) got himself the power over all the other kings. He was called EGBERT. He was very wise, and brave, and handsome ; so the people loved him, and were sorry when he died. His son and then three of his grandsons reigned after him, whose names you will learn another time.

While these men were kings, some strong and cruel heathens, called DANES, came to England, in larger and better ships than the first Saxons came in, and they robbed the people, and burnt the towns, and did more mischief than I can tell you.

I do not know what would have become of England, if a very wise and good king had not begun to rule England about that time. His name was ALFRED. He was the grandson of King Egbert, and was as handsome and brave as his grandfather.

But I must tell you a great deal about King Alfred, which I am sure you will like to hear.

When he was a little boy, his mother wished him to learn to read, and she used to show him beautiful pictures in a book of Saxon poems, and to tell him what the pictures were about. Little Alfred was always pleased when the time came for seeing the book ; and one day, when his mother was talking to him, she said that she would give him the book for his own, to keep, as soon as he could read it. Then he began to take

Alfred learning to read.

pains, and very soon learned to read the book, and his mother kept her promise and gave him the book. When he grew bigger he learned the old Saxon songs by heart, and sang them to his mother, who loved to hear Alfred sing and play the harp.

But when Alfred grew up he had other things to do than reading and singing, for a long time. I told you that the Danes had done a great deal of mischief before Alfred was king ;

and indeed at the beginning of his reign they went on doing quite as much, and he had more than fifty battles to fight, before he could drive them away from his kingdom.

For some years after he was made king he had not one town where the people dared to obey him, for fear of the Danes; and he was obliged to disguise himself in poor clothes, and to live with one of his own cowherds, whose wife did not know the king.

This cowherd lived in a part of Somersetshire, called the Isle of Athelney. While Alfred was there, some of his best friends used to go and tell him how the country was going on, and take messages to him from other friends; and they all begged him to stay where he was till they could collect English soldiers enough to fight the Danes in that neighbourhood.

While he was staying at the cowherd's house, I have heard that the man's wife scolded him one day heartily. I will tell you how it happened.

She had just made some nice cakes for supper and laid them on the hearth to toast, and seeing Alfred sitting in the house doing something to his bow and arrows, she desired him to look after her cakes, and to turn them when they were toasted enough on one side, that they might not be burnt. But Alfred could think of nothing but making ready his bow and arrows to fight against the Danes; he forgot the cakes, and they became very much burnt. When the cowherd's wife came into the house again, she soon saw the cakes on the hearth, quite black and burnt, and began scolding Alfred very severely.

Just then her husband came in with some of Alfred's friends, who told him that they had beaten the Danes, and driven them out of that part of the country, and the people were

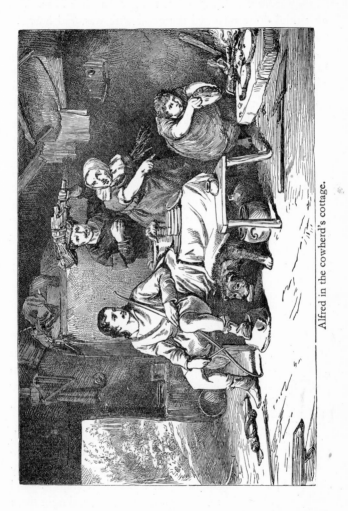

Alfred in the cowherd's cottage.

asking for him, and it was time to appear as their king. You may think how surprised the good wife was, and how she asked the king's pardon for scolding him.

He only smiled, and said, if she forgave him for burning her cakes, he would forgive her for the scolding. Then he thanked her and the cowherd heartily for letting him live so quietly with them, and went with his friends to find the Danes, with whom he had a great deal of trouble before he could drive them away.

At last, when Alfred had overcome the Danes, and when England was at peace, he thought of the great pleasure he had in reading, and determined to encourage all the young people in England to love to study. So he inquired for what learned men there were in England, and sent for more to come from other countries, and paid them for teaching the young men ; and he built several schools.

That he might encourage all his subjects to read, he took the trouble to translate several books for them out of Latin into English ; and, besides that, he wrote several himself for their instruction.

Alfred was never idle. One part of every day was spent in praying, reading, and writing ; one part in seeing that justice was done to his subjects, in making good laws, and in teaching the English how to keep away the Danes from their country. He allowed himself little time indeed for sleeping, eating, and walking about.

One of the very best things King Alfred did for England, was to build a great many ships. He wisely thought that the best means of keeping away the Danes, or any other enemy that could reach England by sea, was to have ships as good as theirs, and go and meet them on the water, and fight them there, instead of allowing them to land and do mischief, and carry away the goods, and sometimes even the children of the people on the sea-coast ; so he built more than a hundred vessels, and he was the first king of England who had good ships of his own.

King Alfred building his Navy.

He may truly be called the Father of our Navy, which has not only made safe our shores and the homes of our race who have settled in countries of their own far over the seas, but has done very much to destroy such evils as slavery about which I shall tell you later, and other forms of cruelty and so has been helpful to the whole world.

Besides fighting the Danes, Alfred made other good uses of his ships. He sent some to Italy and France, to get books, and many things that the English did not then know how to make at home. And other vessels he sent to distant countries, even as far as Russia, to see what the people were like, and if they had anything in their country that it would be useful to England to buy. I have read an account of one of the voyages made by a friend of Alfred's, which the king wrote himself, after his friend had told him what he had seen, and when you are old enough to read it, I dare say it will please you as much as it pleased me.

Alfred died when he had been king twenty-nine years. He was ill for a long time before he died, but he was very patient, and bore great pain without complaining.

Just before he died he spoke to his son Edward, and gave him good advice about taking care of the people when he came to be king.

I will tell you some of the very words he said to Edward. Perhaps you will not fully understand them now, but pray remember them, because, when you are a man you will love to think of them, and to recollect that they were the very words of the best and wisest king we have ever had.

The words are these—

It is just that the English people should be as free as their own thoughts.

CHAPTER X

EDWARD AND ATHELSTANE

As soon as King Alfred died, his son Edward was made king ; and he had soon a great deal to do, for the Danes thought they could conquer all England, now Alfred was dead, and that there would be nobody able to fight them.

But they were mistaken, for King Edward was a brave man and a wise king, although he was not so clever and good as his father, and he kept down the Danes while he was king. He had a sister who helped him in everything. Her husband was dead, and she had no son, so she lived with her brother, and gave him good advice, and took care of one part of the country while he was fighting the Danes in another. You may think how sorry the king was when she died, and how sorry the people were too, for she was good and kind to everybody ; but they were still more sorry when King Edward died soon after, for they were afraid the Danes would get the upper hand again.

The next king was called Athelstane ; he was Edward's eldest son ; he was clever and brave. He knew that it was good for England to have a great many ships, both to keep away the Danes and to fetch cloth and silk from other countries, for the English did not make any of these things then. So he made a law that every man who built a ship and went to sea three times, should be a *Thane*, which means that he would be in the same rank, and be shown the same respect, as one of the landed gentry.

Once I was reading a very old book, and I found something in it about this Athelstane that I will tell you. A king of the Danes and three other kings, who all lived in very cold poor countries, agreed that they would come to England, which was a much better country than their own, and take part of it for themselves ; and they got a great many soldiers to come with them in their ships ; and they watched till King Athelstane's ships were gone out of sight, and then landed, and began to take a part of the country. But Athelstane soon heard of their coming, and called his soldiers together, and went to meet these kings at a place called Brunanburgh, and fought with them, and conquered them, and took some of them prisoners.

One of the prisoners was called Egill, and he told the man who wrote the old book I mentioned to you, that King Athelstane behaved very kindly to all the people after the battle, and would not let even the enemies that were beaten be killed or vexed in any manner, and that he invited him and some of the other prisoners to supper at a large house which he had near the place where the battle was fought.

When they went to supper, they found that the house was very long and broad, but not high, for it had no rooms up stairs, and there was no fire anywhere but in the kitchen and the great hall.

In the other rooms they had no carpets, but the floors were strewed over with rushes, and there were only wooden benches and high stools to sit upon.

The supper was in the great hall. I do not know what they had to eat, but after supper the king asked the company to go and sit round the fire, and drink ale and mead. Now they had no fireplace like ours at the side of the hall ; but there was a great stone hearth in the middle of the floor, and a large fire was made on it of logs of wood bigger than one man could lift, and there was no chimney, but the smoke went out at a hole in the roof of the hall.

When the company came to the fire, King Athelstane made King Egill sit on a high stool face to face with him, and King Athelstane had a very long and broad sword, and he laid it across his knees, so that if any of the company behaved ill he might punish them. And they all drank a great deal of ale, and while they drank several men, called minstrels, sang to them about the great battles they had fought, and the great men who were dead ; and the kings sang in their turn, and so they passed the evening very pleasantly.

The next morning, when Egill and his friends expected to be sent to prison, King Athelstane went to them, and told them he liked such brave and witty men as they were, and that if they would promise not to come to England to plague the people any more, they might go home unharmed. They promised they would not come any more, and then Athelstane let them go home, and gave them some handsome presents.

CHAPTER XI

YEARS OF VIOLENCE

King Athelstane died soon after the battle of Brunanburgh.

His brother Edmund began his reign very well, and the English people were in hopes that they should be at peace, and have time enough to keep their fields in order, and improve their houses, and make themselves as comfortable as they were when Alfred was king. But Edmund was killed by a robber before he had been king quite six years ; and his brother Edred, who was made king when he died, was neither so brave nor so wise as Edmund or Athelstane, and did not manage the people nearly so well.

I am very sorry for the next king, whose name was Edwy, He was young and good-natured, and so was his beautiful wife, whom he loved very much ; but they could not agree with a bishop called Dunstan, who was a very bold man, and wanted everybody in England, even the king, to follow his advice in everything. Now the king and queen did not like this, and would not do everything Dunstan wished, and banished him from the country. But the friends whom he had left behind him rose up against the poor king, and, in order to punish him for not obeying Dunstan, one of them, the Archbishop Odo, was so wicked as to take the beautiful young queen, and beat her, and burn her face all over with hot irons, to make her look ugly, and then he sent her away to Ireland. When she came back, she was so cruelly treated that she died in agony. The men who did this even took

away a part of the kingdom from Edwy, and gave it to his
brother, Edgar. Soon afterwards Edwy died, and Edgar
became king of the whole of England.

When Edgar grew up, he was a good king ; but he was
obliged to make friends with Dunstan, who was clever and
used to please and amuse the people when he wanted them
to do anything for him. He could play on the harp very
well ; and he used to make a great many things of iron and
brass, which the people wanted very much, and gave them
to them ; and as there were no bells to the churches before
this time, Dunstan had a great many made, and hung up in
the church-steeples. And the people began to forget how
cruel he had been to King Edwy, when he did so many things
to please them.

I must tell you a little about King Edgar now. He went
to every part of the country to see if the people were taken
care of. He saw that all the ships that King Alfred and King
Athelstane had built were properly repaired, and built many
new ones. There was so little fighting in his time that he was
called " The Peaceful " ; yet he made the kings of Scotland
and the kings of Wales obey him ; but instead of taking
money from them, as other kings used to do at that time, he
ordered them to send hunters into the woods, to catch and
kill the wolves and other wild beasts, which, as I told you
before, used to do a great deal of mischief in England. I have
heard that he made these kings send him three hundred
wolves' heads every year ; so at last all the wolves in England
were killed, and the farmers could sleep comfortably in the
country, without being afraid that wild beasts would come
and kill them or their children in the night.

This was a very good thing ; and Edgar did many other
useful things for England, but I am sorry to say, he did not

always do what was right, as you will know when you are
old enough to read the large History of England.

When Edgar died, his eldest son, Edward, became king.
Now the queen, who was Edward's stepmother, hated him,

King Edward stabbed by order of Elfrida.

because she wanted her own little son to be king. She therefore determined to have Edward killed ; and I will tell you
how the wicked woman did it. Edward was very fond of
hunting ; one day he was returning alone from the chase,
and being hot and thirsty, he rode up to the gate of his step-

mother's house at Corfe, and asked for some wine. The
queen, whose name was Elfrida, brought him some herself;
and while he was drinking it, she made a sign to one of her
servants, who stabbed Edward in the back, so that he died
almost directly. This cruel murder of the young king, when
he was off his guard, drinking his wine, is said to have given
rise to the custom among noblemen and gentlemen of
" pledging " each other, while drinking at feasts. One about
to drink would call on the guest next him, or on some friend
at the table, to pledge himself to protect him while in the act
of drinking, and he in turn would pledge himself to protect
his friend when the cup came to him. I need not tell you, I
am sure, that after such a wicked action Elfrida was very
unhappy all her life, and everybody hated her. The murdered young king was called Edward the Martyr.

CHAPTER XII

ENGLAND UNDER THE DANES

The son of the wicked Elfrida was king after his brother Edward. His name was Ethelred, and he was king a great many years, but never did anything wise or good. The Danes came again to England, when they found out how foolish King Ethelred was, and that he was never ready, either with his ships or his soldiers, or with good counsel ; for which reason he was called ETHELRED THE UNREADY. I should be quite tired if I were to tell you all the foolish and wicked things that were done, either by this king, or by the great lords who were his friends.

He allowed the Danes to get the better of the English everywhere ; so they robbed them of their gold and silver, and sheep and cattle, and took their houses to live in, and turned them out. They burnt some of the English towns, and altered the names of others ; they killed the people, even the little children ; till at last you would have thought the whole country belonged to them, and that there was no king of England at all. You may think how unhappy the people were then, the cruel Danes robbing and murdering them when they pleased. The king was so idle, that he did nothing to save his people. There was no punishment for bad men, and nobody obeyed the laws.

When Ethelred died, the English hoped they would be happier ; for his son, Edmund Ironsides, was a brave and wise prince, and was made king after his father ; but I am sorry to tell you that he died in a very short time, and then the Danes drove all the princes of England away, and made one of their own princes king of England.

The princes of Alfred's family were forced to go into foreign countries ; some went to a part of France called Normandy, and some to a very distant country indeed, called Hungary.

It was well for England that the Danish king was good and wise. His name was Canute. When he saw how unhappy the people of England were, and how ill the Danes treated them, he was very sorry, and made laws to prevent the Danes from doing any more mischief in England, and to help the English to make themselves comfortable again. And because some of King Alfred's good laws had been forgotten, while the wars were going on, he inquired of the old judges and the wise men how he could establish those laws again, and he made the people use them. Besides this, he restored some of the schools which had been destroyed in the wars, and even sent young men to the English College at Rome to study. So that he did more good to England than any king since Athelstane's time, except King Edgar.

Have you ever heard the pretty story about Canute and his flatterers ?—I will tell it you ; but first you must remember that flattering is praising anybody more than he deserves, or even when he does not deserve it at all. One day, when Canute was walking with the lords of the court by the sea-side, some of them, thinking to please him by flattery, began to praise him very much indeed, and to call him great, and wise, and good, and then foolishly talked of his power, and said they were sure he could do everything he chose, and that even the waves of the sea would do what he bade them.

Canute did not answer these foolish men for some time.

At last he said, "I am tired, bring me a chair." And they brought him one ; and he made them set it close to the water ; and he said to the sea, "I command you not to let your waves wet my feet ! " The flattering lords looked at one another, and thought King Canute must be mad, to think the sea would really obey him, although they had been so wicked as to tell him it would, the moment before. Of course the sea rose as it does every day, and Canute sat still, till it wetted him and all the lords who had flattered him so foolishly. Then he rose up, and said to them, " Learn from what you see now, that there is no being really great and powerful but GOD ! He only, who made the sea, can tell it where and when to stop." The flatterers were ashamed, and saw that King Canute was too good and wise to believe their false praise.

Canute was King of Denmark and Norway as well as England ; and he was one of the richest and most powerful kings, as well as the best, that lived at that time. He reigned in England for nineteen years ; and all that time there was peace, and the people improved very much. They built better houses, and wore better clothes, and ate better food. Besides, they had more schools, and were much better brought up. Canute was kind to learned men, and encouraged the English in everything good and useful.

I am sorry to say, however, that they still had many slaves, instead of servants, to wait upon them, and to help to till the ground for them.

By slaves, I mean men and women who are the property of others, who buy and sell them, as they would horses.

Formerly there were white slaves in almost every country ; afterwards, when white slaves were not allowed by law, people went and stole black men, from their homes and families, and carried them to places so far from their homes, that they could never get back again, and made them work for them. And it is still not a great many years since some kind and true men caused a law to be made that there shall be no more slavery, though in some countries, even now, men and women unhappily are sometimes captured to be sold as slaves.

The reason I tell you about slavery in this place is, that the Danes had many English slaves, and the rich English had many Britons, and even poor English, for their slaves ; for although the Danes and English loved to be free themselves, they thought there was no harm in making slaves of the prisoners they took in battle, or even of the poor people of their own country, whom they forced to sell themselves or their children for slaves, before they would give them clothes or food to keep them from starving. By degrees, however, these wicked customs were left off, and now we are all free.

After wise King Canute's death, there were two more Danish kings in England, one called Harold Harefoot, and the other Hardicanute ; but they reigned a very short time, and did little worth remembering ; so I shall say nothing more about them. In the next chapter we shall have a good deal to learn.

CHAPTER XIII

EDWARD THE CONFESSOR

I told you that when the Danes got so much the better of the English as to make one of their own princes king, they drove away the princes of Alfred's family ; and I told you, at the same time, that some of these princes went to Normandy, which was governed by a duke instead of a king. The duke at that time was brave and generous, and kind to the princes, and protected them from their enemies, and allowed them to live at his court. One of the English princes was called Edward ; and, after the three Danish kings were dead, this Edward was made king of England.

The people were all delighted to have a prince of Alfred's family once more to reign over them ; for, although Canute had been good to them, they could not forget that he was one of the cruel Danes who had so long oppressed the English; and, as to his sons, they never did anything good, as I told you before ; and the people suspected them of having murdered a favourite young prince, called Alfred.

King Edward was very much liked at first ; but he was idle, and allowed sometimes one counsellor and sometimes another to govern him and the kingdom, while he was saying his prayers, or looking over the workmen while they were building new churches.

Now it is very right in everybody to say prayers ; but when God appoints us other duties to do, we should do them carefully. A king's duty is to govern his people well ; he must not only see that good laws are made, but he must also take care that everybody obeys them.

A bishop's duty is to pray and preach, and see that all the clergymen who are under him do their duty, and instruct the people properly.

A soldier's duty is to fight the enemies of his country in war, and to obey the king, and to live quietly in peace. A judge's duty is to tell what the law is, to order the punishment of bad people, and to prevent wickedness. A physician's duty is to cure sick people ; and it is all people's duty to take care of their own families, and teach them what is right and set them good examples.

It has pleased God to make all these things duties, and He requires us to do them ; and He has given us all quite time enough to pray rightly, if we really and truly love God enough to do our duties to please Him. So King Edward, if he had loved God the right way, would have attended to his kingdom himself, instead of letting other people rule it.

However, in King Edward's time, people thought that everybody who prayed so much must be very holy, and therefore after his death he received the name of Edward the Confessor, meaning that he confessed or owned his faults, praying to be forgiven.

One of the great men who ruled England in Edward's time was Godwin, Earl of Wessex. He was clever, and very powerful. After his death, his son Harold became Earl of Wessex, and did all the king ought to have done himself, and tried to keep strangers out of the country.

But King Edward, who had been kindly treated in Normandy, when the Danes drove him out of England, had brought a great many Normans home with him ; and when they saw how pleasant England was, and what plenty of corn,

3

and cattle, and deer there was in it, and how healthy and strong the people grew, they determined to try and get the kingdom for their duke as soon as Edward was dead. And they told the duke what they thought of, and he came from Normandy to see King Edward, and to get him to promise that he should be king of England, as King Edward had no son.

Now I think this was not right, because Edward had a relation who ought to have been king, and his name was Edgar, and he was called the Atheling, which means the Prince.

Perhaps if Edward the Confessor had taken pains to get the great men in England to promise to take care of Edgar Atheling, and make him king, they would have done so ; but as they found he wanted to give England to the Duke of Normandy, a great many of them thought it would be better to have an English earl for a king, because the English earl would be glad to protect his own countrymen, but that a Duke of Normandy would most likely take their houses and lands and give them to the Normans. So they were willing that Harold, the son of Earl Godwin, who already acted as if he were under-king, should be the real king after Edward's death.

In the mean time King Edward was busy in building Westminster Abbey, and encouraging Norman bishops and soldiers to come to England, where he gave them some of the best places to live in.

I must tell you, however, of one very useful thing that was done in the reign of Edward. He found that some part of England was ruled by laws made by King Alfred or other English kings before his time, and some parts by laws made by the Danes, and that the people could not agree about these laws ; so he ordered some wise men to collect all these laws together, and to read them over, and to take the best English laws, and the best Danish laws, and put them into one book, that all the people might be governed by the same law.

William rallies the Normans at Hastings.

King Edward died after he had reigned twenty-two years in England, and the English gave the kingdom to Harold the under-king. But he had a very short reign. As soon as it was known in the North of England that Edward was dead, Harold's brother, Tostig, who had been driven out of his earldom over that part of the country, came back with the King of Norway to fight against Harold. But the other English people joined Harold, and went to battle against Tostig, who was soon killed, and Harold might have been King of all England.

But while Harold was in the North the Duke of Normandy came over to England with a great number of ships full of

Battle of Hastings.

soldiers, and landed in Sussex. As soon as Harold heard of this, he went with his army to drive the Normans away; but he was too late, they had got into the country; and in a great battle fought near Hastings, Harold, the English king, was killed, and the Duke of Normandy made himself king of England.

I do not think the English would have allowed Duke William to be king so easily, if he had not told them that Edward the Confessor had promised that he should be king and persuaded them that the prince Edgar Atheling, who, as I told you, ought to have been king after Edward, was too silly ever to govern the kingdom well.

But after the English Harold was killed, and Edgar Atheling, with his sister, had gone to Scotland, to escape from the Normans, the English thought it better to submit to William, who had ruled his own country so wisely, that they hoped he would be a good king in England.

CHAPTER XIV

WILLIAM I.—1066 TO 1087

A great change was made in England after the Duke of Normandy became king.

All the Normans spoke French, and the English spoke their own language ; so at first they could not understand one another. By degrees the Normans learnt English ; and some of their French words got into our language ; but the old English was for the most part the same as that which you and I speak and write now.

The Normans were used to live in finer and larger houses than the English. So when they came to England they laughed at the long low wooden houses they found, and built high castles of stone for themselves, and made chimneys in their rooms, with the hearth on one side, instead of in the middle of the floor, as I told you the English had it in King Athelstane's time.

There was one law the Normans made, which vexed the English very much.

In the old times, anybody who found a wild animal, such as a deer, or a hare, or a partridge, or pheasant, in his fields or garden, or even in the woods, might kill it, and bring it home for his family to eat. But when the Normans came, they would not allow anybody but themselves, or some of the English noblemen, to hunt and kill wild animals ; and if they found a poor person doing so, they used either to put out his eyes, to cut off his hand, or to make him pay a great deal of money ; and this they called " The Forest Law." I must say I think the new King William behaved very cruelly about this.

He was so fond of hunting himself, although he would not let the poor English hunt, that he turned the people out of a great many villages in Hampshire, and pulled down their houses, and spoilt their gardens, to make a great forest for himself and the Norman barons to hunt it, and that part of the country is still called " The New Forest."

There was another rule which William made, and which the English did not like, but I am not sure whether it was wrong ; and as he made the Normans obey it, as well as the English, it was fair at least.

I must tell you what it was ; he made all the people put out their fires at eight o'clock at night, at the ringing of a church bell, which was called the Curfew Bell. Now, though it might have been of use to some people to keep a fire later, yet, as almost all the houses, both in the towns and the country, were built of wood, it was much safer for everybody to put out the fire early.

I should never have done, if I were to tell you all the changes that were made in dear old England by the Normans. But there is one I must try to explain to you, because it will help you to understand the rest of our history. When William was quite settled in England, which was not till after seven years, when the poor English were tired of trying to drive him and his Normans away, he took the houses and lands from the English thanes and earls, and gave them to the Norman noblemen, who were called barons.

This was unjust. But as the Normans had conquered the English, they were obliged to submit even to this. But William made an agreement with the barons to whom he gave the lands of the old thanes, that when he went to war they should go with him ; that they should have those lands for themselves and their children, instead of being paid for fighting, as soldiers and their officers are now, and that they should bring with them horses and arms for themselves, and common men to fight also.

Some of the barons who had very large shares of land given to them, were bound to take a hundred men or more to the wars ; some, who had less land, took fifty, or even twenty. The greatest barons had sometimes so much land, that it would have been troublesome to them to manage it all themselves ; so they divided it among gentlemen whom they knew, and made them promise to go with them to the wars, and bring their servants, in the same manner as the great barons themselves did to the king.

Now these lands were called feuds, and the king was called the feudal lord of the barons, because they received the *feud* or piece of land from him, and they in return promised to serve him ; and the great barons were called the feudal lords of the small barons, or gentlemen, for the same reason. And when these feuds were given by the king to the great baron, or by a great baron to another, the person to whom it was given knelt down before his feudal lord, and kissed his hand, and promised to serve him. This was called *homage*.

There is only one more thing that I shall tell you about William. He sent people to all parts of England, to see what towns and villages there were, and how many houses and people in them ; and he had all the names written in a book called "Domesday Book." Domesday means the day of judging, and this book enabled him to judge how much land he had, and how many men he could raise to fight for him.

At last King William died. He received a hurt from his

horse being startled at the flames of a small town in France, which his soldiers had set on fire, and was carried to the Abbey of St. Gervase, near Rouen, where he died. He was Duke of Normandy and afterwards King of England, and is sometimes called William the Conqueror, because he conquered English Harold at the battle of Hastings. He was cruel and very passionate ; he took money and land from every one who offended him ; and, as I have told you, vexed the English, and indeed all the poor, very much. And this is being a tyrant, rather than a king.

He had a very good wife, whose name was Matilda, but his sons were more like him than like their mother ; however, you shall read about the two youngest of them, who came to be kings of England, while the eldest, Robert, was Duke of Normandy for a little while.

3*

CHAPTER XV

WILLIAM II.—1087 TO 1100

As soon as William the Conqueror's death was known in England, his second son, William, who was called Rufus, which means the Red, persuaded the noblemen in England to make him king, instead of his elder brother, Robert. I dare say the noblemen were soon sorry they did so; for although none of William the Conqueror's sons were very good, this William Rufus was the worst of all. Robert became Duke of Normandy, but his brother William gave him a great deal of money, to let him govern the dukedom, while he went to fight in the Holy Land, where a great many warriors went to rescue Jerusalem from the Mahometans. These were called *Crusaders*, which means " soldiers of the Cross," and their wars were called the Crusades.

King William Rufus then ruled over Normandy and England too, and behaved as a much worse tyrant than his father.

I must tell you a story about William and his two brothers, Robert and Henry. Robert, the eldest, as I told you, became Duke of Normandy, when William made himself King of England, but they neither of them thought of giving anything to Henry; so he got a good many soldiers together, and went to live in a castle on the top of a high rock, called St. Michael's Mount, close to the sea-shore of Normandy, and he and his soldiers used to come out and plunder the fields of both Robert and William, whenever they had an opportunity. This was wrong in Henry in every way, but chiefly because he robbed and frightened people who had never done him any harm, and had nothing to do with the unkindness of his brothers.

Well, Robert and William collected an army, and went to his castle, to drive him out, and they contrived to keep him so closely confined, that neither he nor his people could get out to fetch water. Robert and William heard of this, and that the people in the castle were dying of thirst. William was very glad, because he said they would soon get the castle ; but Robert, who was more generous, immediately gave his brother Henry leave to send and get as much water as he wanted ; and besides that, sent him some of the best of his own wine. Henry soon after gave up the castle.

This story shows you how cruel William was to his own brother ; so you may think he did not behave better to his subjects, and that they were not very sorry when he was killed by accident. Some tell the story of his death in this manner :—One day when he was hunting in the New Forest, made by his father, which you read about in the last chapter, he had a gentleman named Walter Tyrrel with him, who was reckoned skilful in shooting with a bow and arrow. This gentleman, seeing a fine deer run by, wished to show the king how well he could shoot ; but he was a little too eager, and his arrow, instead of going straight to the deer, touched a tree, which turned it aside, and it killed the king, who was standing near the tree. But the truth is that it was never known who shot the arrow that killed the king.

Some poor men found William's body lying in the forest, and carried it to Winchester, where it was buried.

William Rufus does not deserve to be remembered for many things, yet we must not forget that he built a good bridge over the river Thames, just where the old London bridge stood, till it was taken down, when the fine new bridge was finished; besides that, he built Westminster Hall, near the Abbey, and when you walk to Westminster you will see part of the very wall raised by him. But its large and beautiful roof was built three hundred years later by Richard the Second.

CHAPTER XVI

HENRY I.—1100 TO 1135

As soon as the nobles and bishops knew that William Rufus was dead, they determined that his younger brother, Henry, should be king, because Robert, the eldest, was too busy about the wars in the Holy Land, which I mentioned before.

Now Henry was brave and clever, like his father, but he was not quite so cruel.

He was very fond of books, and encouraged learned men, and his subjects gave him the name of Beauclerc, which means fine scholar. He married Matilda, whose uncle was Edgar Atheling, who ought to have been King of England after Edward the Confessor. The English people were pleased to have her for their queen, because they hoped she would make Henry more kind to them than his brother and father had been ; and they called her " the good queen Maude " (which is short for Matilda). She had two children, William and Maude ; but William was not at all like his good and kind mother, who died when he was a boy. He loved to drink wine, and was very quarrelsome ; and he used to say that, if ever he became king, he would treat the English worse than they had ever been treated before ; so nobody but the Normans cared for him. But he never came to be king, as I will tell you.

He had been with his father into Normandy, and when they were to return, instead of coming in the same ship with his father, he chose to come in one called the White Ship, where there were a number of foolish young people like himself. They amused themselves so long ashore, drinking before they set off, that they were a great way behind the king, who got safe to England. The prince and his companions had drunk so much wine, that they did not know what they were about, so that the White Ship ran on a rock, and, not being able to manage the vessel properly, they were all drowned. I have read that Prince William might have been saved, but he tried to save a lady who was his near relation, and in trying to save her he was drowned himself; and this is the only good thing I know about Prince William. You may think how sorry King Henry was to hear that his only son was drowned.

Indeed, I have read that nobody ever saw him smile afterwards. He had lost his good wife, and his only son, and now he had nobody to love but his daughter Maude.

When Maude was very young, she was married to the German Emperor, Henry the Fifth; but he died very soon; however, people always called her the Empress Maude. And then her father made her marry a nobleman, named Geoffrey, who was Count or Earl of Anjou; and she had three sons, the eldest of whom came to be one of the greatest of our kings.

Now I told you King Henry Beauclerc was very fond of his daughter. Her eldest son was named Henry, after him; and he meant that his daughter Maude should be Queen of England after he died, and that her little Henry should be the next king.

But he was afraid that the Norman barons would not like to obey either a woman or a little child, and that they would make some grown-up man of the royal line king instead; and he did everything in his power to make all the barons promise to make Maude queen after his death. But they would not all promise ; and I am sorry to say that some of those who did forgot their promise as soon as he was dead, and took the part of Stephen, as I will tell you by and by.

While Henry was busy, doing all he could to make his daughter queen, he died.

I must tell you the cause of his death ; for I think it is a good lesson to all of us. He had been told by the physicians that he ought not to eat too much, but one day a favourite dish was brought to his table (I have read that it was potted lampreys), and he ate such a quantity that it made him ill, and so he died, after he had been king thirty-five years.

CHAPTER XVII

STEPHEN—1135 TO 1154

As soon as Henry the First was dead, his nephew Stephen, who was handsome, and brave, and good-natured, was made king. A great many Norman barons, and English lords and bishops, went with him to Westminster Abbey, and there the Archbishop of Canterbury put a crown upon his head, and they all promised to obey him as their king. But the other barons, and lords, and bishops, who, as I told you before, had promised to obey the Empress Maude as Queen of England, and to keep the kingdom for her young son Henry, sent to fetch them from Anjou, which was their own country, and tried to make her queen. I am sorry to say that the friends of Stephen and the friends of Maude began to fight, and never ceased from doing so for fifteen years.

This fighting was very mischievous to the country ; whole towns were destroyed by it ; and while the war between Stephen and Maude lasted, the corn-fields were laid waste, so that many people died for want of bread ; the flocks of sheep and herds of cattle were killed, or died for want of care ; the trees were cut down, and nobody planted young ones ; and there was nothing but misery from one end of the kingdom to the other. This sort of war between two parties of the people of the same country is called civil war, and it is the most dreadful of all warfare.

If strangers come to fight, and all the people of a country join to drive them away, the mischief they may have done is soon repaired ; and the people of a country love one another the better because they have been defending one another.

But in a civil war, when people in the same country fight, it is not so. The very next door neighbours may take different sides, and then the mischief they may do one another will be always remembered, and they will dislike one another even after peace is made.

I have heard things so dreadful about civil wars, you would hardly believe them. It is said even that two brothers have taken different sides in a civil war, and that when there was a battle it has happened that one brother has killed the other, and when he found out what he had done, he was ready to kill himself with grief. Only think how dreadful such a thing is, and how sorry the father and mother of those brothers must have been !

These sad wars lasted more than fifteen years ; at last everybody got tired of them, and it was settled by some of the wisest of the barons and bishops that Stephen should be king as long as he lived ; that Maude should live in Anjou ; and that when Stephen died, her son Henry should be king of England.

Stephen did not live very long after this agreement was made. He had some good qualities, but the wars, which troubled all England while he reigned, prevented their being of much use. He was King of England for nineteen years.

CHAPTER XVIII

HENRY II.—1154 TO 1189

We have so much to learn about King Henry the Second, that I think I must divide the account of his reign into two chapters.

In the first, I will write all the best things I remember; and in the second, all the bad. Some things that are middling will be at the end of the good, and some at the end of the bad chapter.

It was a glad day for England when young Henry, the son of Maude, was made king. He was wise and learned, and brave and handsome, besides being the richest king of his time, and having the largest estates.

The first thing he did when he was king was to send away all the Norman and French soldiers who had been brought to England to fight either for Stephen or for Maude. He paid them their wages, and sent them to their own homes, along with their captains, because he thought English soldiers were best to defend England, and that foreign soldiers were not likely to be kind to the poor English people.

He next made the barons, whether Norman or English, pull down a great many of their castles, because robbers used to live in them, and, after they had robbed the farmers of their cattle or corn, they used to hide themselves in these castles, and the judges could not get at them to punish them.

Then King Henry built up the towns that had been burnt in the wars of Stephen, and sent judges to do justice all through the land, and the people began to feel safe, and to build their cottages, and plough the fields ; and the country was once more fit to be called dear merry England.

Instead of fighting and quarrelling with one another, the young men used to make parties together, and ride out with their dogs, to hunt the foxes and deer in the forests ; and sometimes the ladies went with them, to see a kind of sport that was very pretty, but it is not used now. Instead of dogs, to catch wild animals, they used a bird called a hawk to catch partridges and pigeons for them. It took a great deal of trouble to teach the hawks, and the man who taught them and took care of them was called a Falconer, because the best kind of hawk is the falcon.

When the ladies and gentlemen went hawking the falcons used to sit upon their left wrists while they held a little chain in their hands ; and there was a hood over the falcons' heads, that their eyes might be kept clear. As soon as the party got into the fields they took the hood off the birds' eyes, and as soon as they saw any game they loosed the little chain they held in their hands, and then the falcons flew after the game ; and the ladies and gentlemen rode up after them to receive the game when the falcons had caught it.

King Henry loved hunting very well, but he was too wise to hunt much. He spent most of his time in going about to see what wanted mending after the sad civil war we read of in the last chapter ; and he employed the cleverest men he could find to put everything in order, and made the wisest men judges ; and he got some learned men to seek out all the best laws that had ever been made in England ; and, as the long wars had made the people forget the laws, he ordered the judges to go to all the towns by turns several times a year, and do justice among all the English.

King Henry was very fond of learning, and gave money to learned men and to those who made verses, or as we call them poets ; and by and by I dare say you will read about one that Henry was kind to, named Wace, who wrote a poem about the ancient Britons, and another about the ancient Normans.

Before I can tell you of a thing that was partly good and partly bad for England in this King Henry's reign, I must put you in mind that I have told you nothing yet about IRELAND, the sister-island of Great Britain. It was never conquered by the Romans ; and the people were as ignorant as the Britons before the Romans came, with just the same sort of houses and clothes. They might have been in the same state for many years if a very good man, whom the Irish called Saint Patrick, had not gone from Britain to Ireland and taught the people to be Christians ; and he and some of his companions also taught them to read ; and the Irish people began to be a little more like those in other parts of the world.

Ireland was divided into several kingdoms ; and, in King Henry's time, their kings quarrelled sadly with one another. And one of them came to Henry, and begged him to go to help him against his enemies. But Henry had too much to do at home. However, he said that, if any of his barons liked to go and help the Irish king, they might. And the Irish king, whose name was Dermot, promised that if they could punish or kill his enemies, he would call the King of England Lord over Ireland, and that he and the rest of the Irish kings should be his servants.

Then the Earl of Strigul, who was called Strongbow, and some other noblemen, gathered all their followers together, and went to Ireland to help Dermot ; and, after a great deal of fighting, they conquered that part of Ireland opposite to England, and drove the people over to the other side; just as the English had driven the Britons to Wales. From that

Dermot, King of Leinster, doing homage to Henry II.

time Ireland has always been under the same king with England.

You remember, I am sure, that one part of Britain is called Scotland. Now, at the time I am writing about, Scotland had kings of its own, and was more like England than any other country ; but it was much poorer, and the people were ruder and wilder.

The king of Scotland, named William the Lion, having heard that King Henry was in Normandy, thought it would be a good opportunity to take an army into England, to rob the towns and carry away the corn and cattle ; and so he did. But several of the noblemen and bishops got together a number of English soldiers and marched to the North, and fought King William and took him prisoner.

William was sent to London, and King Henry would not set him free till he had promised that, for the future, the kings of Scotland should be only under-kings to the kings of England ; and from that time the kings of England always said Scotland was theirs ; but it was long before England and Scotland became one kingdom.

I do not think this was quite good for England, though the English drove the Scots home again, because it made many quarrels and wars between England and Scotland. As I have now mentioned the best part of Henry the Second's reign, we must end our long chapter.

CHAPTER XIX

HENRY II.—(*continued*)

It is a pity that we must think also of the bad things belonging to Henry's reign.

I dare say you remember the chapter in which I told you how the Angles and Saxons became Christians, and that a bishop of Rome sent Augustine and some companions to teach the people. Now the bishops of Rome called themselves popes, to distinguish themselves from other bishops; and, as most of the good men who taught the different nations to be Christians had been sent from Rome, the popes said they ought to be chief of all the bishops and clergymen in every country.

This might have been right, perhaps, if they had only wanted to know that everybody was well taught. But they said that the clergymen were their servants, and that neither the kings nor judges of any country should punish them, or do them good, without the pope's leave. This was foolish and wrong. Although the clergymen are in general good men, because they are always reading and studying what is good, yet some of them are as wicked as other men, and ought to be judged and punished for their wickedness in the same manner.

And so King Henry thought.

But the Archbishop of Canterbury, whose name was Thomas Becket, thought differently.

This Becket wanted to be as great a man as the king, and

tried to prevent the proper judges from punishing wicked clergymen, and wanted to be their judge himself. And there were sad quarrels between the king and Becket on that account.

At last, one day, after a very great dispute, Henry fell into a violent passion, and said he wished Becket was dead. Four of his servants, who heard him, and wished to please him, went directly to Canterbury, and, finding Archbishop Becket in church, they killed him with great cruelty.

You may think how sorry King Henry was that he had been in such a passion ; for, if he had not, his servants would never have thought of killing Becket. It gave the king a great deal of trouble before he could make the people forgive the murder of the archbishop. And this was one of the very bad things in Henry's life.

There was another bad thing, which perhaps caused the king more pain than the killing of Becket. It was owing, mostly, to something wrong which the king had been persuaded to do when he was very young.

You shall hear. I told you how very rich King Henry was ; the thing that first made him so was his early marriage to one of the richest ladies in the world, although she was very ill-tempered, and in all ways a bad woman. It is said that she was handsome ; but I am sure she must have been wicked, for she was once married to a French king, who found her out in such wicked actions, that he sent her away, and gave her back all her money and estates, as he did not choose to have so bad a wife.

Now Henry, instead of choosing a good wife, when he was only nineteen years old married this bad woman for her riches.

Her name was Eleanor of Aquitaine, and they had four

sons, Henry, Richard, Geoffrey, and John. She brought up these children badly, and, instead of teaching them to love their father, who was very kind to them, she encouraged them to disobey him. When her son Henry was only sixteen, she told him he would make a good king, and never rested till his good-natured father caused him to be crowned king, and trusted a great deal more to him than was right ; till at last young Henry became so conceited that he wanted to be king altogether, and, by the help of this wicked mother, and of the king of France, he got an army and made war against his father.

However, he did not gain anything by his bad behaviour, and soon afterwards he became very ill, and died without seeing his father ; and, when he was dying, he begged his servants to go and say to the king his father that he was very sorry indeed for his wickedness, and very unhappy to think of his undutiful behaviour. The king was even more unhappy than the prince had been, for he loved his son dearly.

I am sorry to say the other three sons of Henry and Eleanor did not behave much better. Richard was as violent in temper as his mother, but he had some good qualities, which made his father hope he might become a good king when he himself was dead. But Queen Eleanor, with the help of the King of France, contrived to make Richard and his brother Geoffrey fight against their father. As for John, though he was too young to do much harm himself while King Henry lived, yet he became as wicked as the rest when he grew up. Geoffrey married Constance, Princess of Brittany, but he died soon after. He had only one son, named Arthur, about whom I will tell you more in a short time.

Now Henry's great fault, in marrying a bad woman because she was rich, brought the greatest punishment with it, for she taught her children to be wicked, and to rebel against their father. And there is nothing in the world so unhappy as a family where the children behave ill to their parents.

I beg now, my dear little Arthur, that you will take notice, that all the good belonging to Henry's reign concerns the country. While he was doing his duty, being kind to his subjects, repairing the mischief done in the civil wars, and taking care that justice was done, and that learning and learned men were encouraged, he was happy.

His bad actions always hurt himself. If he had not given way to his passion, Thomas Becket would not have been killed by his servants, and he would not have suffered so much sorrow and vexation.

And if he had not married a woman whom he knew to be wicked, his children might have been comforts to him instead of making war upon him; and they might have been better kings for England after his death.

Henry the Second has often been called Henry Plantagenet. His father was the first person in his family to whom that name was given, and I will tell you why.

When people went to battle long ago, to keep their heads from being wounded, they covered them with iron caps, called helmets; and there were bars like cages over their faces, so that their best friends did not always know them with their helmets on. Therefore, they used to stick something into their caps, by which they might be known; and Henry's father used to wear in his helmet a branch of broom, called planta genista, or shortly Plantagenet; and so he got his name from it.

CHAPTER XX

RICHARD I.—1189 TO 1199

You remember that Henry the Second's eldest son, Henry, died before his father; his second son, Richard, therefore, became King of England. He was called Richard of the Lion's Heart, because he was very brave.

Now, in the time when King Richard lived, people thought a great deal more of kings who fought, and conquered large kingdoms, than of those who tried to make their own people happy at home in a small kingdom. And so it was in England. People really began to forget all the good their late wise king, Henry Plantagenet, had done, and to like Richard Plantagenet better, because he told them he would go to war, and do great feats of arms at a great distance, and that he would not only make his own name famous, but that their dear England should be heard of all over the world; and that, when he, and the English gentlemen and soldiers who would go with him, came back, they would bring great riches, as well as a great deal of fame. By fame, I mean that sort of praise which is given to men for bravery, or wisdom, or learning, or goodness, when they are a great deal braver, or wiser, or more learned, or better than other people.

Now, of all these qualities, bravery is the least useful for kings; yet I believe that their people as well as themselves often like it the best—at least it was so with Richard. He had no sooner invited the English to go to the wars with him, than the nobles who had the large feuds, or fiefs, that I told

you of in the chapter about William the Conqueror, and the
gentlemen who had the small fiefs under the nobles, and all
their servants, made ready to go.

And they went to the same wars that William the Conqueror's son, Robert, went to ; for those wars, which were
called Crusades, lasted a long time, but I cannot give you an
account of them now. So I will tell you what happened in
England when Richard and the best noblemen and soldiers
were gone.

First of all, many of the wise rules of King Henry were
broken, as soon as the people found there was no king in
England to watch over them. Then, as the barons had taken
away not only all their own money, but also that of the
farmers and townspeople from whom they could borrow
any, everybody was poor, and some people were really
starved. Many of those who could not find any employment
turned robbers, and plundered the people ; and the judges
were not able to punish them, because the king had taken all
the good soldiers with him, and there was nobody to catch
the robbers and bring them before the judges.

There was a very famous robber in those times, called
Robin Hood. He had his hiding-place in the great forest of
Sherwood, in the very middle of England. He only robbed
rich lords or bishops, and was kind to the common people,
who liked him, and made merry songs about him, and his
three friends, Friar Tuck, Little John, and Allan-a-Dale.

Then there was another bad thing owing to Richard's
being in the wars so far off. He was often wanting money
to pay his soldiers, and the English, who were proud of their
brave king, in spite of all they suffered from his being so far
away, used to sell anything they had for the sake of sending
the king what he wanted. This was very right, while they

only sent their own money. But there happened at that time to be a great many Jews in England : these unfortunate people, who had no country of their own, lived at least in peace while wise Henry was king. They were very industrious, and taught the English many useful things. They were the best physicians and the best merchants in the country. But the people were jealous of them for their riches, and they did not like their strange dress, nor their strange language. So now, when there was no king in England to protect these Jews, they fell upon them, and robbed them of their money and goods, which they pretended they meant to send to Richard. But most of the money was kept by Prince John and some of the worst of the barons, who had stayed at home ; and they encouraged the people to treat the Jews very cruelly, besides robbing them, and they killed a great many. I am sure that, when you are old enough to read of the bad treatment of the Jews at York, you will be ashamed to think such cruel things could have been done in England.

There was one person less to blame for the bad things done at this time than might have been expected ; I mean Queen Eleanor.

She behaved as well to her son Richard as she had behaved ill to her husband, and while he was at the wars she tried hard to persuade her youngest son, John, not to rebel against Richard, as he was striving to do. All the foolish and all the wicked barons, both Norman and English, followed Prince John ; but there were enough good barons to defend Richard, though he was so far off ; and a good many bishops joined them, and prevented John from making himself king.

When Richard of the Lion's Heart, as he was called on account of his great courage, heard how much the people of England were suffering, he resolved to come home ; but as he was coming the shortest way, one of his enemies contrived to take him prisoner, and to shut him up in a castle, so that it was a long time before anybody knew what had become of the King of England.

King Richard I. made prisoner by the Duke of Austria.

That enemy was Leopold, Duke of Austria, with whom Richard had quarrelled when they were at the Crusade. Now Richard, who was really good-natured, although he quarrelled now and then, had forgotten all about it; but

Leopold was of a revengeful temper, and as soon as he had an opportunity he took him, as I have told you, to a castle in his country ; but he had soon to give him up to his lord, the Emperor, who imprisoned him in a strong tower.

In old times a beautiful story was told about the way the English found out where Richard was. It was this. Richard had a servant called Blondel, who loved his master much. When Richard did not come home, Blondel became very anxious, and went in search of him. He travelled from one castle to another for some time, without finding his master. At last one evening, when he was very tired, he sat down near the castle of Trifels to rest, and while he was there he heard somebody singing, and fancied the voice was like the king's. After listening a little longer, he felt sure it was, and then he began to sing himself, to let the king know he was there ; and the song he sang was one the king loved. Some say the king made it. Then Richard was glad, for he found he could send to England, and let his people know where he was.

This is the old story. But it was in another way that the people in England heard of the captivity of their king. The moment they did so, they determined to do everything they could to get him home. They sent to the Emperor to beg him to set Richard at liberty ; but he said that the English should not have their king until they gave him a great deal of money ; and when they heard that, they all gave what they could ; the ladies even gave their gold necklaces, and ornaments of all kinds, to send to the Emperor that he might set Richard free.

At length the king came home ; but he found that while he was away, Philip, King of France, had been making war on his subjects in Normandy ; and, besides that, had been helping his brother John to disturb the peace in England ; so he went to Normandy to punish Philip very soon afterwards, and was killed by an arrow shot from a castle called Chaluz, when he had only been king ten years.

Many people praise and admire Richard of the Lion's Heart, because he was so brave and hardy in war. For my part, I should have liked him better if he had thought a little more about taking care of his own country ; and if he had stayed in it and done justice to his people, and encouraged them to be good and industrious, as his wise father did.

CHAPTER XXI

JOHN—1199 TO 1216

John, the youngest son of Henry Plantagenet, became king after the death of his brother Richard.

His reign was a bad one for England, for John was neither so wise as his father, nor so brave as his brother. Besides, he was very cruel.

At first he had been called John Lackland, because his father had died before he was old enough to get possession of the lands that his father wished to give him. And not long after he became king he lost Normandy and all the lands that had belonged to his grandfather, Geoffrey of Anjou. He did not know how to govern England so as to repair the ill it had suffered while Richard was absent at the wars, so that the Pope called upon the King of France to go to England, and drive John away and make himself king instead ; and then John was so base that he went to a priest called a Nuncio, or Ambassador, who came from Rome, and really gave him the crown of England, and promised that England should belong to the Pope, if the Pope would only keep him safe.

You cannot wonder that John was disliked ; but when I have told you how he treated a nephew of his, called Prince Arthur, you will, I am sure, dislike him as much as I do. Some people thought that this Prince Arthur ought to have been King of England, because he was the son of John's elder brother, Geoffrey. And John was afraid that the barons and

4

other great men would choose Arthur to be king, so he contrived to get Arthur into his power.

He wished very much to kill him at once ; but then he was afraid lest Arthur's mother should persuade the King of France and the other princes to make war upon him to avenge Arthur's death. Then he thought that, if he put out his eyes,

Prince Arthur and Hubert.

he would be so unfit for a king, that he should be allowed to keep him a prisoner all his life ; and he actually gave orders to a man named Hubert de Burgh to put his eyes out, and Hubert hired two wicked men to do it.

But when they came with their hot irons to burn his eyes out, Arthur knelt down and begged hard that they would do anything but blind him ; he hung about Hubert's neck, and kissed and fondled him so much, and cried so bitterly, that neither Hubert nor the men hired to do it could think any more of putting out his eyes, and so they left him.

But his cruel uncle, John, was determined Arthur should not escape. He took him away from Hubert, and carried him to a tower at Rouen, the chief town of Normandy, and shut him up there.

One night, soon afterwards, it is said that Arthur heard a knocking at the gate ; and when it was opened, you may think how frightened he was to see his cruel uncle standing there, with a servant as bad as himself, whose name was Maluc ; and he was frightened with reason ; for the wicked Maluc seized him by the arm, and stabbed him in the breast with his dagger, and then threw his body into the river Seine, which was close to the tower, while King John stood by to see it done.

It was for this wicked action that his grandfather's estates in France, as well as the dukedom of Normandy, were taken away from King John.

For his faults in governing England so badly, he had a different punishment. All his subjects agreed that, as he was so cruel as to put some people in prison, and to kill others, without any reason, instead of letting the proper judges find out whether they deserved punishment or not, they must try to force him to govern better. And for this purpose the great barons and the bishops, and gentlemen, from all parts of England, joined together, and they sent word to John, that, if he wished to be king any longer, he must promise to do justice, and to let the English people be free, as the English kings had made them before the Conquest.

At first, John would not listen to the message sent by the barons, and would have made a civil war in the country ; but

he found that only seven of the barons were his friends, and there were more than a hundred against him. Then he said that if the greatest barons and bishops would meet him at a place called Runnymede, near Windsor, he would do what they wished for the good of England. And they met the king there ; and, after some disputing, they showed him a sheet of parchment, on which they had written down a great many good laws, to prevent the kings of England from being cruel and unjust, and to oblige them to let the people be free.*
King John was very much vexed when he read what they had written ; but as he could not prevail upon them to let him be their king, if he did not agree to do what they wished, he put his seal at the end of the writing, and so he was obliged to do as the barons desired him to do.

This parchment is called the Great Charter, in English. Most people call it by its Latin name, which is Magna Carta. Now you must remember this name, and that King John put his seal upon it at Runnymede—because it is of great consequence, even to us who live now, that our king should keep the promises John made to the English people at Runnymede.

A good king would have been glad to promise these things to his people, and would have liked to keep his word. But as John was passionate and greedy, it vexed him very much not to be allowed to put people in prison, or to rob them of their money or their houses, when he pleased.

If John had been honest, and had tried to keep his word, he might have lived happily in England, although he had lost Normandy. But he was always trying to cheat the people and the barons, and did not keep the promises he made in Magna Carta ; and he made everybody in England so

* If little Arthur has forgotten what I mean by the people being free, let him read the eighth chapter over again.

angry, that they allowed the King of France's son to come to England, and make war upon John. So that all the rest of his reign was unhappy; for although many of the barons helped him to defend himself from the French prince, when

King John granting Magna Carta.

the Pope, who now thought that England belonged to him, ordered them to do so, they never could trust him, and he died very miserably, knowing that he was disliked by everybody.

CHAPTER XXII

HENRY III.—1216 TO 1272

The reign of John's son, who was called Henry the Third, was very long and wretched. He was made king when he was only nine years old, and there were civil wars for almost fifty years while he lived.

You must think that such a little boy as Henry was, when he was made king, could not do much for himself, or anything at all for his subjects. But he had a wise guardian, called the Earl of Pembroke, who did many things to repair the mischief done by King John. However, that wise man died very soon, and then the king behaved so ill that there was nothing but quarrelling and fighting for the greater part of his life.

I think you do not know what TAXES are ; I must tell you, that you may understand some things you must read about in History.

TAXES are the money which subjects pay to the king, or to those persons who govern his kingdom for him.

I must now tell you why taxes are paid. Every man likes to live safely in his own house ; he likes to know that he and his wife, and his children, may stay there without being disturbed, and that they may go to sleep safely, and not be afraid that wild beasts, or wicked men, or enemies like the old Danes, may come and kill them while they are asleep. Next to his life and the lives of his wife and children, a man likes to know that his money and his furniture are safe in his house, and that his horses and cows, and his trees and his corn-fields, are safe out of doors.

Now he could never have time to watch all these things himself, and perhaps he might not be strong enough to fight and drive away the wicked men who might try to rob or kill him ; so he gives money, which he calls taxes, to the king, who pays soldiers and sailors to keep foreign enemies away, and policemen to watch the streets and houses, to keep away thieves and robbers ; besides, he pays the judges to punish men who are found doing anything wrong.

So you see that whoever wishes to live safely and comfortably ought to pay some taxes.

Sometimes it happens that a king spends his money foolishly, instead of putting it to the good uses I have mentioned, and then wishes to get more, even by unjust means. And this is what King Henry and his father, King John, were always trying to do. And they were so wicked as to rob their subjects, many of whom they put into prison, or threatened to kill, if they did not give them all they asked for, and that was the beginning of the miserable civil wars in the time of Henry the Third.

The whole story of these wars would be too long for us now. So I will only tell you that one of the bravest men that fought against the king was Simon de Montfort, who was a very wise man ; and although he was killed in a great battle, he had forced the king and parliament, before he died, to observe a custom which is most useful even to us who live now.

It is this :—No king can make his subjects pay a tax without the consent of the parliament. Now, though several kings tried, after this time, to get money by some other means than these, the people would never allow them to do so, and their only trying to do it always did themselves a great deal of mischief, as you will read by and by.

And I want you to remember that Simon de Montfort was the first man in England that called the people in the towns to send members to parliament. This was in the year 1265. The common people loved him so much that, when he was dead, they called him Sir Simon the Righteous.

I am afraid this is a very dull chapter, but you see it is very short.

CHAPTER XXIII

EDWARD I.—1272 TO 1307

When the unhappy King Henry the Third died, his eldest son Edward was abroad, fighting in the same country where I told you William the Conqueror's eldest son Robert went, and where Richard of the Lion's Heart spent the greatest part of his reign. When he heard his father was dead he came home, and brought with him his very good wife, Eleanor of Castile, who had saved his life in Syria, by taking great care of him when he was wounded.

Edward was crowned king as soon as he came to England ; he was as wise as Henry the Second, and as brave as King Richard of the Lion's Heart.

His wisdom was shown in the manner in which he governed his people. His bravery everybody had seen before he was king, and he showed it afterwards in fighting against the Welsh and the Scots, which I will tell you about by and by.

While Edward was a young man, he travelled a great deal into different countries, and whenever he saw anything done that he thought good and right he remembered it, that he might have the same thing done in England when he was king.

When he was in Spain he married his good wife Eleanor ; and as her father and brother were wise kings, he learned a great many useful things from them.

One thing was, how to take care of cows and horses much

4*

better than the English had done before ; and another thing
was, to improve the gardens and fields with many kinds of
vegetables for eating, and with new sorts of grass for the
cattle. In return for what he learned in Spain he sent some
good sheep from England to that country, because the sheep
they had before were small, and had not such fine wool as
our sheep ; but since the English sheep went to feed among
the Spanish hills their wool has been some of the best in the
world.

When King Edward came home to England, he determined to do everything he could to make the people happy :
he knew they could not be happy if the laws were not
obeyed ; so he was determined that no wicked person should
escape without punishment, and that all good people might
live quietly, and do what they liked best.

I told you before that wise Simon de Montfort, who was
killed in Henry the Third's reign, had got the king to observe
the custom of not taking money from the people without the
consent of the parliament. This law King Edward improved
very much, and he improved the parliament too.

Edward, who was very wise, thought that, as there were a
great many more towns than there used to be in the olden
times, and a great many more people in all the towns, it
would be a good thing if some of the best men belonging to
the largest towns came to the parliament. The largest towns
in England were then called burghs, and the richest men who
lived in them were called burgesses, and King Edward settled
that one or two burgesses out of almost every burgh should
come along with the great noblemen, and the bishops, and
the gentlemen to the parliament. I told you in the last chapter
that Simon de Montfort did this once ; but Edward first made
it the rule.

These burgesses made the parliament complete. In the first place, there was the king to answer for himself; in the second place, the great lords and bishops to answer for themselves; and, thirdly, the gentlemen and burgesses to answer for the country gentlemen and the farmers and the merchants and the shopkeepers. For a time the clergy also sent persons to act for them; but they soon gave up doing so.

So King Edward the First made good rules about the parliament, which were not much changed for a very long time. Besides that, he improved the laws, so as to punish the wicked more certainly, and to protect the lives and goods of everybody. And in these things Edward was one of the best kings that ever reigned in England.

We will end this chapter here, while we can praise King Edward the First—who was, as I told you, wise and brave, and very handsome; but people used to call him Longshanks, because his legs were rather too long.

CHAPTER XXIV

EDWARD I.—(*continued*)

I am afraid I must not praise King Edward so much, now we are come to his wars, for twice he was very cruel indeed.

You remember that the old Britons were driven by the Angles and Saxons out of England into different countries, and that most of them went to live among the mountains in Wales, where the conquerors could not easily get to them.

These Britons chose princes of their own : one to reign over them in North Wales, one in South Wales, and one in Powys, which was between the two. Many of these princes were very good rulers of the country, and protected it from all enemies, and improved the people very much, by making good laws.

I am sorry to say, however, that the princes of the different parts of Wales sometimes quarrelled with one another, and very often quarrelled with the English who lived nearest to Wales. They did so while Edward was King of England, and he went to war with them, as he said only to make their princes come to him and do him the homage that the Welsh princes had done in former times. But, finding that he could very easily conquer the first of them with whom he fought, he determined to get all Wales for himself, by degrees, and to join it for ever with England.

Llewellyn was the last real Prince of Wales before it was taken by the English kings. He loved a young lady called Elinor de Montfort very much, for she was good and beautiful, and he intended to marry her. She was the daughter of the brave Simon de Montfort who fought against Henry the Third. She had been staying a little while in France, and was coming to Wales in a ship, and was to be married to Llewellyn as soon as she arrived. Unhappily, King Edward heard of this, and sent a stronger ship to sea, and took the young lady prisoner, and shut her up in one of his castles for more than two years, and would not let the prince see her until he should do him homage.

Llewellyn fought a great many battles to defend his native land. At last he had no part of Wales left but Snowdon and the country round it. Then he yielded to Edward, who gave him Elinor de Montfort to wife. But he soon began to fight again, hoping that he might by degrees get the better of the English, but at the last he was killed by a soldier, who cut off his head and took it to King Edward, who was then at Shrewsbury.

Edward was so glad to find that Llewellyn was dead, that he forgot how unbecoming it is for a really brave man to be revengeful, especially after an enemy as brave as himself is dead ; and I am sorry and ashamed to say that, instead of sending the head of Llewellyn to his relations, to be buried with his body, he sent it to London, and had it stuck up over one of the gates of the city with a wreath of willow on it, because the Welsh people used to love to crown their princes with willow.

Soon after the death of Llewellyn, his brother David was made prisoner by the English. Edward treated him with still greater cruelty than he had treated Llewellyn, and, after his head was cut off, set it up over the same gate with his brother's.

It has been said, that because the *bards* or poets of Wales

used to make verses, and sing them to their harps, to
encourage the Welshmen to defend their country and their
own princes from Edward, he was so cruel as to order them
all to be put to death. I hope it is not true.

Death of Llewellyn, last of the Welsh Princes.

For two hundred years Wales was in a sad state. The
English kings did not rule it wisely ; for they did not treat
the Welsh so well as they did the English. The Welsh,
therefore, feeling this to be very unjust, were often trying to

set up princes for themselves. But at last, a king of Welsh descent, named Henry the Eighth, thought it right to make the Welsh and English equal : and from that time they have lived happily together.

We must now speak of King Edward's wars in Scotland.

I told you that, while Henry the Second was king, William, King of Scotland, had made war in England ; and after being taken prisoner and brought to London, Henry had set him free, on his promising that the kings of England should be lords over the kings of Scotland.

Now, it happened that while Edward the First was King of England, Alexander, King of Scotland, died, and left no sons. The Scots sent to fetch Alexander's granddaughter from Norway, where she was living with her father, King Eric, that she might be their queen. But the poor young princess died.

Two of her cousins, John Baliol and Robert Bruce, now wanted to be king ; but as they could not both be so, they agreed to ask King Edward to judge between them ; and King Edward was very glad, because their asking him showed the people that they owned he was Lord of Scotland, and he chose John Baliol to be king of Scotland.

You will read the story of all that John Baliol did in the History of Scotland.

Edward watched Scotland very narrowly, and when any Scotsman thought that King John had treated him unjustly, he would appeal for justice to Edward, who said that, as he was Lord of Scotland, he would take care that Scotland was governed properly ; till at last John Baliol went to war with Edward ; but he was beaten, and the richest and best part of Scotland was taken by Edward. He was very severe, nay cruel, to the Scots.

At last a gentleman named Sir William Wallace could not bear to have the Scots so ill treated as they were by the English governors that Edward sent into the country. So he went himself, or sent messengers, to all the barons and gentlemen he knew, to beg them to join him, and drive the English out of Scotland ; and they did so, and might have made their own country free, if Sir William Wallace had not been taken prisoner and carried to London, where King Edward ordered his head to be cut off, which was as wicked and cruel as his cutting off the heads of the two Welsh princes.

This did not end the war in Scotland ; for another Robert Bruce, who had come to be king after Baliol, determined to do what Sir William Wallace had begun ; I mean, to drive the English out of Scotland ; and he made ready for a long and troublesome war, and King Edward did the same ; but when Edward had got to the border of Scotland with his great army, to fight King Robert, he died.

If King Edward the First had been content to rule over his own subjects, and to mend their laws, and encourage them to trade and to study, he would have made them happier ; and we who live now should have said he deserved better to be loved.

Indeed, he did so much that was right and wise, that I am sorry we cannot praise him in everything.

His greatest fault was ambition—I mean, a wish to be above everybody else, by any means. Now, ambition is good when it only makes us try to be wiser and better than other people, by taking pains with ourselves, and being good to the very persons we should wish to get the better of.

But when ambition makes us try to get things that belong to others, by all means, bad or good, it is wrong.

Ambition caused wise King Edward to forget himself, after conquering the Prince of Wales, and to take Wales as if it were his own country, that there might never be greater men in Wales than the kings of England.

The ambition to be King of Scotland made Edward go to war with the Scots, and made him so cruel as to cut off the head of Sir William Wallace, because he wanted to save his country from being conquered by Edward.

So you see ambition led Edward to do the two most cruel actions he was ever guilty of.

CHAPTER XXV

EDWARD II.—1307 TO 1327

Edward the Second was made king after his father's death. He is often called Edward of Caernarvon, because he was born at a town of that name in Wales. He was the first English prince who was called Prince of Wales.

Since his reign the eldest son of the King of England has almost always been called so.

Edward of Caernarvon was the most unhappy man that ever was King of England.

And this was in great part his own fault.

He was very fond of all kinds of amusements, and instead of taking the trouble, while he was young, to learn what was good and useful for his people, so as to make them happy, he spent all his time in the company of young men as idle and as foolish as he was. One of the first of these was called Pierce Gaveston. Edward the First had sent that young man away, and on his death-bed begged his son not to take him back again, for he would be sure to lead him into evil ways. But the prince was obstinate, and chose to have him with him.

After Edward of Caernarvon became king this same Gaveston caused him a great deal of trouble. He made the king quarrel with his nobles, who were very haughty and fierce, and did not like to see the king always in the company of foolish young men.

Moreover, the queen, Isabella of France, was very proud and hot-tempered, and did not strive to make the king better, as she might have done had she been gentle and amiable.

The nobles were greatly vexed because Edward spent all the money they had given to his father in making presents to Gaveston and his other companions, so they joined together and made war upon the king. There was civil war for many years ; and so many wicked things were done in that war, that I am sure you would not wish me to tell them. It ended by Gaveston being killed by order of the barons.

This civil war was hardly over before the king made war against Robert Bruce, the King of Scotland, and went with a large army into Scotland ; but he was beaten at the battle of Bannockburn in such a manner that he was glad to get back to England, and to promise that neither he nor any of the kings of England would call themselves kings of Scotland again.

You would think that Edward would now have been wise enough neither to vex the barons and the people by spending the money trusted to him foolishly, nor to make himself disliked by choosing bad companions. But I am sorry to say he did not grow wiser as he grew older, and the queen behaved very foolishly and wickedly. The king chose a favourite of the name of Spenser ; the queen's chief friend was a baron named Mortimer.

Very soon there was another civil war : the queen kept her eldest son Edward, the Prince of Wales, with her, and said she only fought against the king for his sake ; and that if she did not, the king would give so much to Spenser that he would leave nothing for the prince.

At last the queen and her friends took the king prisoner. They shut him up in a castle called Berkeley Castle. They gave him bad food to eat, and dirty water to drink and to wash himself with. They never let him go into the open air to see any of his friends. This poor king was very soon murdered. The queen's favourite, Mortimer, being afraid the people would be sorry for Edward, when they heard how ill he had been used, and might perhaps take him out of prison and make him king again, sent some wicked men secretly to Berkeley Castle, and they killed the king in such a cruel way that his cries and shrieks were heard all over the castle.

He had been king twenty years, but had not been happy one single year.

CHAPTER XXVI

EDWARD III.—1327 TO 1377

When poor Edward of Caernarvon was murdered, his son, Edward, who had been made king in his place, was only fourteen years old.

Queen Isabella and her wicked friend Mortimer ruled the kingdom, as they said, only for the good of young King Edward. But, in reality, they cared for nothing but their own pleasure and amusement, and behaved so ill to the people, that the young king's uncles and some other barons joined together against Mortimer. But he was too strong for them, and beheaded one of the king's uncles.

At last the young king had the spirit to seize Mortimer, and he was hanged for a traitor. Queen Isabella was put in prison ; but as she was the king's mother, he would not have her killed, although she was so wicked, but gave her a good house to live in, instead of a prison, and paid her a visit every year as long as she lived. Thus, the young King Edward the Third, at eighteen years old, took the kingdom into his own hands, and governed it wisely and happily.

In many things he was like his grandfather, Edward the First. He was wise and just to his own subjects. He was fond of war, and sometimes he was cruel.

I must tell you a little about his wife and children, before we speak of his great wars.

His wife's name was Philippa of Hainault. She was one of the best and cleverest and most beautiful women in the world.

She was very fond of England, and did a great deal of good to the people. A great many beautiful churches were built in Edward's reign, but it was Queen Philippa who encouraged the men who built them. She paid for building a college and new schools in Oxford and other places. She invited a French clergyman, named Sir John Froissart, to England, that he might see everything, and write about it in the book he called his Chronicles, which is the most amusing book of history I ever read. Queen Philippa and her son, John of Gaunt, who was called the Duke of Lancaster, loved and encouraged Chaucer, the first great English poet. By and by, when you are a little older, you will like to read the stories he wrote. Besides all this, there were some good men who wished to translate the Bible into English, so that all the people might read and understand it. The leader of these good men was John Wiclif, the first great reformer of religion in England. In this reign the great people began to leave off talking Norman French and to talk English, almost like our English now. And the king ordered the lawyers to conduct their business in English instead of French.

Queen Philippa had a great many children, all of whom she brought up wisely and carefully. Her eldest son Edward was called the Black Prince, it is said because he used to wear black armour. He was the bravest and politest prince at that time in the world ; and Queen Philippa's other sons and her daughters were all thought better than any family of princes at that time.

We must now speak of the king and his wars. These wars made him leave England, and go to foreign countries very often ; but as he left Queen Philippa to take care of the country while he was away, everything went on as well as if he had been at home.

Soon after Edward became King of England, Charles, King of France, who was Edward's uncle, died. And as Charles had no children, Edward thought he had a right to be King of France, rather than his cousin Philip, who had made himself king on Charles's death. The two cousins disputed a good while as to who should be king. At last, as they could not agree, they went to war, and this was the beginning of the long wars which lasted for many kings' reigns between France and England.

In that time, a great many kings and princes, and barons, or, as they began to be commonly called, nobles, did many brave and generous deeds, and gained a great deal of honour for themselves, and glory for their country ; but the poor people, both in England and France, suffered a great deal. The English parliament was so pleased that our kings should overcome the French, that they allowed the king to have such great taxes to pay the soldiers with, that the people could hardly keep enough to live upon. And the French people suffered more, because, besides paying taxes, the armies used to fight in their land, and the soldiers trampled down the corn in the fields, and burned their towns and villages, and often robbed the people themselves. And so it must always be in a country where there is war. If the captains and officers are ever so kind, and the soldiers ever so good, they cannot help doing mischief where they fight.

In the next chapter I will tell you of two or three of the chief things that happened while King Edward was at war with France.

CHAPTER XXVII

EDWARD III.—*(continued)*

You have heard, I am sure, that the English are famous for being the best sailors in the world, and for gaining the greatest victories when they fight at sea. At the beginning of Edward's French war he gained the first great battle that had been fought at sea by the English, since the times when they had to drive away the Danes : it was fought very near a town called Sluys, on the coast of Flanders. Instead of guns to fire from the ships, they had great stones for the men to throw at one another when they were near enough, and bows and arrows to shoot with from a distance. This was indeed a great battle ; the English and the French never before had fought by sea with so many men and so many and such big ships ; and so I have told you of it.

Besides this sea-fight, there were two great victories won by King Edward on land, which are among the most glorious that have ever been gained by the English. The first was the battle of Crecy.

The French had three times as many men as the English at Crecy, so King Edward knew he must be careful how he placed his army, that it might not be beaten. And he took care that the soldiers should have a good night's rest, and a good breakfast before they began the battle ; so they were fresh, and ready to fight well.

Then the king sent forward his dear son, Edward the Black Prince, who was only sixteen years old, to begin the fight.

It was about three o'clock in the afternoon, on a hot summer's day, when the battle began, and they fought till dark. At one time, some of the gentlemen near the prince were afraid he would be overcome, and sent to his father to beg him to come and help him. The king asked if his son was killed or hurt. "No," said the messenger. "Then," said the king, "he will do well, and I choose him to have the honour of the day himself." Soon after this, the French began to run away, and it is dreadful to think how many of them were killed.

Two kings who had come to help the King of France, one of the king's brothers, and more French barons, gentlemen, and common soldiers than I can tell you, were killed. But very few English indeed were slain. When the King of England met his son at night, after the great battle of Crecy was won, he took him in his arms, and cried, "My brave son! Go on as you have begun! You are indeed my son, for you have behaved bravely to-day! You have shown that you are worthy to be a king." And I believe that it made King Edward happier to see his son behave so bravely in the battle, and so modestly afterwards, than even the winning of that great victory.

A year after the battle of Crecy, the city of Calais, which you know is in France, on the coast just opposite to Dover, in England, was taken by Edward.

The people of Calais, who did not wish their town to belong to the King of England, had defended it almost a year, and would not have given it up to him at last, if they could have got anything to eat. But Edward's soldiers prevented the market people from carrying bread, or meat, or vegetables, into the city, and many people died of hunger before the captain would give it up.

I am sorry to tell you that Edward, instead of admiring the

citizens for defending their town so well, was so enraged at them, that he wanted to have them all hanged ; and when his chief officers begged him not to be cruel to those who had been so faithful to their own king, he said he would only spare them on condition that six of their best men should bring him the keys of the city gates, that they must come bare-headed and bare-footed, with nothing but their shirts on, and with ropes round their necks, as he meant at least to hang them.

When the people of Calais heard this, the men and women, and even the children, thought it would almost be better to die of hunger, than to give up the brave men who had been their companions in all their misery. Nobody could speak.

At last Eustace de St. Pierre, one of the chief gentlemen in Calais, offered to be one of the six, then another of the richest citizens, and then four other gentlemen came forward, and said they would willingly die to save the rest of the people in Calais. And they took the keys, and went out of the town in their shirts, bare-headed and bare-footed, to King Edward's tent, which was a little way from the city gates.

Then King Edward called for the headsman, and wanted him to cut off the heads of those gentlemen directly ; but Queen Philippa, who was in the tent, hearing what the king had ordered, came out suddenly, and fell upon her knees, and would not get up till the king promised to spare the lives of the six brave men of Calais. At last Edward, who loved her very dearly, said, " Dame, I can deny you nothing ; " and so he ordered his soldiers to let the good Eustace de St. Pierre and his companions go where they pleased, and entirely forgave the citizens of Calais.

The second great victory which made King Edward's name

so glorious was that of Poitiers. It was gained about ten years after the battle of Crecy.

King Philip of France, with whom Edward had quarrelled, was dead, and his son John, who was called the Good, had become King of France. Edward went to war again with him, to try to get the kingdom for himself, and at first he thought he might succeed.

The Black Prince was in France with a small army, and reached a place near Poitiers before he met the King of France, who had a great army, with at least five men for every one that was with Edward.

But Prince Edward followed the example his father had set him at the battle of Crecy : he placed his soldiers very skilfully, and he took care that they should have rest and food. The battle began early in the morning, and ended as the battle of Crecy did, by the greater number of the French running away, and a great many of their best gentlemen and soldiers being killed.

But the chief thing that happened was, that King John of France and his youngest son were taken prisoners, and brought to the Black Prince's tent, where he was resting himself after the fight. Prince Edward received King John as kindly as if he had come to pay him a visit of his own accord. He seated him in his own place, ordered the best supper he could get to be made ready for him, and waited on the king at table as carefully as if he had not been his prisoner. Then he said everything he could to comfort him ; and all the time he was with him he behaved with the greatest kindness and respect.

When Prince Edward brought his prisoner, the King of France, to London, as there were no carriages then they rode on horseback into the city. King John was well dressed and

mounted on a beautiful white horse which belonged to the
prince ; while Edward himself rode by his side upon a black
pony to wait upon him and do anything he might want.
And in that manner he went with King John to the palace

Edward the Black Prince waiting on John, King of France.

belonging to the King of England called the Savoy. King
John was set free when peace was made ; but the French
never could afford money enough to pay the English what
they asked for letting him go back to his people. So the good

King John came back, to keep his word of honour, and died in England.

This goodness and gentleness of the Black Prince made everybody love him. And his bravery in battle, and his wisdom in governing those parts of France which his father and he had conquered, gave the English hopes that when he became king he would be as good a king as his father, and that England would be still happier.

But the Black Prince died at the age of forty-six, just one year before his father. His good mother Philippa had died some years before. And all the people of England grieved very much. Their good queen, their favourite prince, and their wise and brave King Edward the Third, all died while the Black Prince's son was quite a child. And though some of the prince's brothers were brave and clever men, the people knew, by what had happened in former times, that the country is never well ruled while the king is too young to govern for himself.

CHAPTER XXVIII

RICHARD II.—1377 TO 1399

Richard the Second was only eleven years old when his grandfather, King Edward the Third, died. He was made king immediately. The people, who loved him for the sake of his good and brave father, the Black Prince, were peaceable and quiet in the beginning of his reign. But his uncles, who were clever men, and wanted to be powerful, did not agree very well with one another.

When Richard was about sixteen, a civil war had very nearly taken place. I will tell you how it happened.

The king was not so well brought up as he ought to have been, and he loved eating and drinking and fine clothes, and he made a great many feasts, and gave fine presents to his favourites, so that he often wanted money before it was the right time to pay the taxes. It happened, as I said, when the king was about sixteen, that he wanted money, and so did his uncles, who were in France, where the French and English still continued to fight now and then. The great lords sent the men who gathered the king's taxes round the country, and one of them, whose business was to get the poll-tax, that is, a tax on everybody's head, was so cruel, and so rude to the daughter of a poor man named Wat Tyler, that Wat, who could not bear to see his child ill-used, struck him on the head with his hammer and killed him.

Wat Tyler's neighbours, hearing the noise, all came round, and, finding how much the tax-gatherer had vexed Wat, they

Death of Wat Tyler.

took his part, and got their friends to do the same, and a great many thousands of them collected together at Blackheath, and sent to the king, who then lived in the Tower of London, to beg him to listen to their complaints, and not to allow the noblemen to oppress them, nor to send to gather taxes in a cruel manner. The king did not go to them, but he read the paper of complaints they sent, and promised to do his people justice. A few days afterwards, the king, with his officers, met Wat Tyler, and a great many of the people who had joined him, in Smithfield, and spoke with him about the complaints the people had made. The Mayor of London, who was near them, fancied Wat Tyler was going to stab the king, so he rode up to him and killed him.

Wat Tyler's friends now thought it best to make peace with the king; so for this time the civil war was stopped.

I have told you this story, to show you what mischief is done by cruelty and injustice. It was unjust to collect the taxes at a wrong time, and for a bad purpose. It was cruel in the tax-gatherer to behave ill to Tyler's daughter. That injustice and cruelty brought about the death of the tax-man, and that of Wat Tyler, who seems to have been a bold, brave man, wishing to do what was right.

Soon after this disturbance, the king was married to a princess of Bohemia, who was so gentle and kind to the people, that they called her the good Queen Anne, and they hoped that she would persuade the king to send away his bad companions; but they were disappointed, for Richard was too ill-tempered to take her advice, and the people, who had loved him when he was a child for his father's sake, now began to hate him.

In the mean time he was at war with Scotland, and with Ireland, and with France; and instead of gaining battles, and

making the name of our dear England glorious, he lost, by
degrees, all credit, and was laughed at by foreigners, as well
as by his own subjects.

I have told you that the king had several uncles, who took

Henry of Hereford claiming the Crown of England.

care of the kingdom while he was a child. Instead of being
grateful for this, he ordered one to be put to death, and ill-
used another ; and when his third uncle, John of Gaunt,
Duke of Lancaster, died, he took all his money and lands
away from John's son, whose name was Henry of Hereford,

5

and made use of his riches to spend in eating, drinking, and riot of all kinds.

The good Queen Anne died soon, and she had no son, and the people all began to wish they had another king instead of this Richard, who was a disgrace to his good father, the Black Prince.

Now Henry of Hereford, who was the king's cousin, was very clever ; and the people knew he was very brave, for he had fought in the armies of some foreign princes at one time. Besides, he behaved kindly and good-naturedly to the people, so a good many of them began to wish him to be king. Then Richard grew afraid of him and sent him out of the country.

Soon word was sent to Henry that King Richard was gone to Ireland to quiet some disturbance there, and that, if he pleased to come to England and make himself king, he would find many persons ready to take his part.

Henry came accordingly, and, on King Richard's return from Ireland, he forced him to call the parliament to meet him in London. Now the lords and the gentlemen, or, as they began to be called, the commons of the parliament, all agreed that Richard was too cruel, and revengeful, and extravagant to be king any longer, and that his cousin, Henry of Hereford, son of the great Duke of Lancaster, should be king.

Richard was forced to give up the crown ; and of all the people who had lived with him, and to whom he had shown kindness, there was only one, the Bishop of Carlisle, who took his part, or said a word in his favour ; so he was put into prison at Pomfret Castle, and some time afterwards he died there. Some people say he was killed by a bad man called Exton ; others say he was starved to death.

CHAPTER XXIX

HENRY IV.—1399 TO 1413

I think that Henry of Hereford did not act rightly in taking the kingdom from his cousin Richard ; but he became a good king for England. He was the first king of the family of Lancaster, and is sometimes called Henry of Lancaster.

During the fourteen years Henry was king he was chiefly busy in making or improving laws for the people.

He had little foreign war to disturb him ; but the Welsh and Scottish several times made war upon the English who lived nearest to them. There was in Henry's days a very famous Scottish earl called James of Douglas, and he came into the north of England and began to burn the villages, and rob the people, until the Earl of Northumberland, whose name was Percy, and his son, Henry Hotspur, gathered their soldiers together, and went to fight Douglas, at a place called Holmedon, and they beat him, and took a great many prisoners.

In those days it was the custom for everybody to do as they pleased with the prisoners they took. A cruel man might kill them, another might make slaves of them ; one a little kinder might say, " If your friends will send me some money, I will let you go ; " but the kindest of all would let them go home again without paying for it.

Now King Henry had a dispute with Earl Percy about those Scottish prisoners, and Percy and his son were so affronted, that they determined to make a civil war, and they were joined by several English lords ; but the person who helped them most was a Welsh gentleman, named Owen Glendower, who was related to the old princes of Wales.

He was very angry with King Henry the Fourth, because he thought he behaved ill to Wales, which was his own country ; besides, he had been a friend of poor Richard the Second ; and though he might have thought it right to keep him in prison, he could not bear to think of his having been put to death.

These reasons made him join the Percys, and they collected a very large army to fight against King Henry. The earl Percy's son was called Harry Hotspur, because he was very impatient, as well as very brave. Indeed, he and the young Prince of Wales, who was called Henry of Monmouth, were the two bravest young men in England. The king's army met the army that Percy and Owen Glendower had raised against him near Shrewsbury, and then everybody thought a great deal about the two young Harrys, who were both so brave and handsome. The battle was fought, and the king gained the victory. Henry of Monmouth behaved as bravely as the Black Prince used to do, and he was not hurt in the battle. Harry Hotspur was equally brave, but he was killed. Oh ! civil war is a sad thing. There was one of the finest young noblemen in England killed among Englishmen, who ought to have agreed, and helped, and loved one another, instead of fighting.

Perhaps you will wonder why I mention the young nobleman particularly, when so many other Englishmen were killed ; and you will wonder if it is of any use that there should be noblemen.

I think it is, and I will tell you why. The first noblemen were those men who had either been very good in all things, or who had found out something useful for everybody, or who had been very brave in battle, or wise in giving good advice.

These their companions called Nobles, and paid them great respect, and gave them more lands, and goods, and money, than other people. And in the Bible you read that the names of those men who do rightly shall be remembered. Now when a man has been made a noble, and his name is remembered because he is good, or manly, or clever, or brave, or wise, his sons will say to themselves, " Our dear father has been made a noble, because he was good or brave ; we must be good or brave, or useful too, that people may see that he taught us well, and that we know how to love and honour him, by following his good example." Then their children will think of how good both their father and grandfather were, and that they will not do anything that they would not have liked, and so they will try to keep the good and noble name, one after another, as it was given to the first of their grandfathers. If the young nobles do this properly, you know they will always be ready to do good to their country, by helping to make good laws, and to do justice in time of peace, and to fight for the safety and glory of their own land in time of war, as their fathers did. Then they will say to themselves, " I am noble and rich, and other people will look up to me ; I must, therefore, try to be better than others, that I may set a good example to the young, and that those who are old enough to remember my father and grandfather, may think I have done as well as they did."

The noblemen made King John do justice to the people, and give them the good laws written in the Great Charter. The noblemen prevented the foolish kings Henry the Third and Richard the Second from doing a great deal of mischief, and they helped our good kings Henry the Second, Edward the First, and Edward the Third to do all the good and useful things I have told you of. So you see that noblemen have been of great use in England. And every one of us, if only in simplicity and good will, may be noble too.

Henry the Fourth died at Westminster, when he had been king only fourteen years. He was wise and just, except in one thing ; and that was, that he punished persons who did not agree with the bishops about the proper way to worship God. Some good men, called Lollards, who loved to read the Bible in English, were put in prison, and otherwise were ill-used, on that account.

CHAPTER XXX.

HENRY V.—1413 TO 1422

I think you would have liked King Henry the Fifth who was often called Harry of Monmouth.

He was good-natured and gay, yet, when it was right to be grave and wise, he could be so, and we never had a braver king in England.

I must tell you a little about his behaviour while he was a young man, and only Prince of Wales, before I say anything about the time when he was king.

It is said that he was merry and fond of playing wild pranks with gay and reckless young men of low birth ; but all the stories told about his conduct at this time can hardly be true. I will tell you some of them.

Once, when he had been doing something wrong, his father, who was ill at Windsor, sent for him, and he went directly in a very droll dress, that he had made for some frolic ; it was of light blue satin, and it had a great many odd puckers in the sleeves, and at every pucker he made the tailor leave a bit of blue thread and a tag like a needle. When the king saw such a strange coat, he was a little vexed that he should dare to come to him wearing it, while he was so ill. But Prince Harry said he was in such a hurry to see his father, and to do whatever he wished, that he could not spare time to take off the coat, and so he came in it just as he was ; and his father forgave him because of his obedience.

Another time he was strolling about in London with some

idle merry companions, when he heard that one of his
servants had behaved ill, and had been carried before the chief
judge, whose name was Sir William Gascoyne. He went
directly to the court where the judge was, and desired him
to let his servant go, just because he was the king's son. But
the judge refused, and said he was sitting there for the king
himself, to do justice to everybody alike, and he would not
let the man go till he had been punished. The prince was in
too great a passion to think rightly at that moment, and he
struck the chief justice. That wise and good man instantly
ordered the officers to take the bold young prince to prison,
and it was not till he had made very humble excuses that he
forgave him, and set him free. He said that such an act was
worse in the king's son than in anybody else ; because, as
he was sitting in the court for the king, other people, if they
offended, were only subjects doing wrong, but the prince,
being the king's son, as well as his subject, was offending both
king and father. Harry had the sense to understand this, and
when his passion was over he thanked the judge, promised
never to behave so ill again, and kept his word.

The king, you may be sure, was pleased with the judge,
who was not afraid to do justice on his son ; and he praised
his son for getting the better of his passion, and submitting
to the judge without complaining. I must tell you, however,
that Gascoyne was removed from being chief justice soon
after Henry became king, but that was because he had grown
old and was no longer fit to do the duty of a judge.

When King Henry the Fourth died, the people may have
been a little afraid lest Harry should not make a good king,
though he might be a merry one. If they were they soon
saw they were mistaken.

None of our kings was more wise, or clever, or brave, or

fonder of doing justice than he ; and even now nobody in England ever thinks of Henry the Fifth without loving him.

In the beginning of his reign there was a war with France. The poor King of France was mad. His queen was a wicked woman, and his son very young. All the noblemen were quarrelling with one another, and the whole together with the King of England.

So Henry made ready his army, and sailed over to France, and, after having taken a town called Harfleur, met a large French army at a place called Agincourt.

The English soldiers were tired with a long march ; they had had very bad weather to march in, which made many of them ill, and they had not enough to eat. But they loved the king ; they knew he was as badly off as they were, and he was so kind and good-humoured, and talked so cheerfully to them, that in spite of hunger, and weariness, and sickness, they went to battle in good spirits. The English bowmen shot their long arrows all at once with such force, that the French soldiers, especially those on horseback, were obliged to give way ; and in a short time King Henry won as great a victory at Agincourt, as Edward the Third and the Black Prince had done at Crecy and Poitiers. One day, when you are older, you will read a most delightful play written by the poet Shakespeare about this battle, and some other parts of King Henry the Fifth's life.

Not long after the battle, Henry went to Paris, and there the princes and nobles told him that, if he would let the poor mad King Charles be called king while he lived, Henry and his children should be always Kings of France. And so peace was made, and Henry governed France for a little while, and he married the French Princess Catherine, and they had a little son born at Windsor, who was called Henry of

5*

Windsor, Prince of Wales, and was afterwards King Henry the Sixth.

Very soon afterwards King Henry the Fifth was taken very ill at Paris. He knew he was going to die, so he sent for his brothers and the other English lords who were in France, and gave them a great deal of good advice about ruling England and France, and begged them to take care of his little son. He then told his chaplain to chant some of the psalms to him, and died very quietly.

The English people wept and lamented bitterly, when they found that they had lost their king.

He was kind to them, and so true and honest, that even his enemies trusted entirely to him. He was handsome, and so good-humoured, that everybody who knew him liked his company ; so good and just, that wicked men were afraid of him ; so wise, that his laws were the fittest for this people that could have been made at the time ; so brave, that the very name of Henry, King of England, kept his enemies in fear. And above all this, he was most pious towards God.

CHAPTER XXXI

HENRY VI.—1422 TO 1461

Henry of Windsor, the poor little Prince of Wales, was not a year old when his father died. He was made King of England directly, and became King of France soon after.

The parliament that his wise father left gave good guardians and protectors to the little king, and to England and to France.

The war in France began again, for the mad king having died, his son, who was almost as good for France as our Henry of Monmouth had been for England, began to try to get back all his father's kingdom. However, the Duke of Bedford, uncle to the little King of England, managed so well for the English, that it really seemed as if France was always to be subject to the King of England.

It was fortunate, for the good of both countries, that it was not to be so.

When the people of France were so tired of war, that they were not able to fight longer, and the king himself had lost all hope of getting back his kingdom, one of the strangest things happened that I ever read about.

A young woman called Joan of Arc, who was the daughter of a tenant-farmer at Domremy in France, had heard a great many people talk about the sad state of all the country, and the great unhappiness of the young French Prince Charles. She thought about this so much, that at last she came to believe that God had sent her to help the Prince to get back his kingdom, and to drive the English out of France.

So she dressed herself like a young man, and got a sword and spear, and went to Chinon, a castle where the prince was, and there she told him, and the few French nobles who were with him, that, if they would only follow her when they were next attacked, they would overcome the English and recover their kingdom.

I should tell you, that the eldest son of the King of France was called the Dauphin, as the eldest son of the King of England is called Prince of Wales.

Well, at first the Dauphin and his friends thought that Joan was mad, but she began to talk to them so wisely, that they listened to her. She cheered the Dauphin, who seemed quite without hope of saving his kingdom ; she said that he ought to call himself king directly, and go to Rheims, where all the kings of France used to be crowned, and have the crown put upon his head, that the people might know he was king.

She told the nobles that the English, if they conquered France, would take away their estates and make them beggars ; that it was shameful to let the poor young Dauphin be driven from the kingdom of his forefathers ; and that they deserved to lose the name of nobles if they were afraid to fight for their own country and king.

Then she went among the common soldiers and the poor people. She said God would have pity on them, if they would fight bravely against the English, who were strangers, and who only came to France to take all that was good from them, and spoil their towns, and trample down their corn, and kill their king, and make beggars of them all.

So by the time the French and English met again in battle, the French had recovered their spirits. And when the king, and the nobles, and the people saw that young woman go in front of the army, and into every dangerous place, although she never would use her sword to kill or wound with, they would have been ashamed not to follow her ; so that her bravery and her good advice did really begin to save her country.

The French drove the English army away from Orleans, and Joan of Arc has been called the Maid of Orleans ever since.

The Maid of Orleans next persuaded the Dauphin to go and have the crown set on his head, and so become really the king ; and as soon as that was done, a great many people came to him, and he very soon had a large army, with which his generals and Joan drove the English out of the greater part of France.

It was a grand sight when Charles the Dauphin went to Rheims, and was crowned, while all the nobles stood by, and the Maid of Orleans close to him, holding the white flag of France in her hand. Some have said that she set the crown on his head and I hope that was true.

I am sorry to tell you the end of the brave Maid of Orleans. She was taken prisoner by the English, and kept in prison for some time. At last, after a long and painful trial by a court of Churchmen presided over by a Bishop of that part of France called Burgundy, they were so cruel as to burn her alive, because they believed she was a witch. But since then we have rightly honoured her for her pure spirit and great courage and her devotion to what she thought was right.

Soon after this the Duke of Bedford died, and by degrees the English lost everything in France but a very little corner of the country, out of all that Henry the Fifth had conquered.

I shall end this chapter here, because we have nothing more to say about France for a long while ; but we shall have to read of some sad civil wars in England, which began at this time.

CHAPTER XXXII

HENRY VI.—(*continued*)

Henry the Sixth grew up to be a pious but very weak man. He was married to a beautiful lady called Margaret of Anjou, who was fierce and cruel, and who behaved more like a passionate man than a woman. She wanted to govern the kingdom entirely herself; and as the only person she was afraid of was the king's uncle, Humphrey, the good Duke of Gloucester, it is supposed that she agreed with Cardinal Beaufort and another person, who hated Duke Humphrey, and that they had him put to death.

Soon after this, as the queen and her friends behaved so ill, several of the noblemen, most of the gentlemen in parliament, and the people in London, began to think it would be better to take away the crown from the poor king, who was too silly to govern for himself, and was often so ill that he could not even speak for days together.

The person they wished to make king was his cousin the Duke of York.

I have read, that some gentlemen were walking together in the Temple garden after dinner, and disputing about the king and the Duke of York; one of them took the king's part, and said, that, though he was silly, his little son Edward, who was just born, might be wise; and he was determined to defend King Henry and his family, and desired all who agreed with him to do as he did, and pluck a red rose, and wear it in their caps, as a sign that they would defend the family of Lancaster.

The gentlemen who thought it would be best to have the Duke of York for their king turned to a white-rose bush, and each took a white rose, and put it in his cap, as a sign he loved the Duke of York ; and for more than thirty years afterwards the civil wars in England were called the Wars of the Roses.

At first, the party of York only wished Richard, Duke of York to be the king's guardian, and govern for him ; and as Duke Richard was wise and good, it might have been well for England if he had been allowed to do so.

But Queen Margaret raised an army to keep away the Duke of York, and the first battle between the people of the Red Rose and the people of the White Rose was fought at St. Alban's.

The Yorkists gained the victory, and there was quiet for a few years. Then another battle was fought, and the queen, with the little prince, went to Scotland, and for some time the Duke of York ruled the kingdom with the king's consent.

However, the queen found means to come back to England, and to gather another great army, with which she fought the Duke of York's army several times, and at last beat them, at a place called Wakefield Green. She cut off the Duke of York's head, and stuck a paper crown upon it, and put it over one of the gates of York.

Could you have thought a woman would be so cruel ?

One of her friends, called Clifford, did something still worse. He saw a handsome youth of seventeen, along with an old clergyman, who was his tutor, trying to get away to some safe place after the battle : he asked who he was, and when the child said he was Rutland, the Duke of York's son, the fierce Clifford stabbed him to the heart with his dagger, although the poor youth and his good tutor fell upon their knees and begged for mercy.

When the people knew of these two cruel things they began to hate Queen Margaret, and a great many went to the Duke of York's eldest son, Edward, and desired he would make himself king.

Now this Edward was brave and handsome, and loved laughing and merriment, but he was sometimes cruel and was too fond of pleasure. However, he was better than Margaret, and the people in London chose him to be king, and so there were two kings in England for ten years ; one, the King of the White Rose, that was Edward ; and one, the King of the Red Rose, that was poor Henry.

CHAPTER XXXIII

EDWARD IV. OF YORK—1461 TO 1483

In those years, while there were two kings, nobody knew which king to obey. Few people minded the laws, and the armies of the Lancastrians and the Yorkists did a great deal of mischief in every part of the country. A great many battles were fought, and many thousands of Englishmen were killed.

After one of these battles, which was fought at Towton, in Yorkshire, King Henry was obliged to hide himself for a long time in Scotland, and the parts of England close to it. He sometimes slept in the woods, and sometimes in caves, and was often near dying of hunger.

At last Queen Margaret contrived to gather another army ; but the Yorkists beat her at Hexham, and King Henry was taken prisoner, and sent to the Tower. Queen Margaret and the young prince escaped into a wild forest, where they were met by some robbers, who took away the queen's necklace and her rings, and then began to quarrel about who should have the most.

Queen Margaret took the opportunity of their quarrelling, and, holding her little son by the hand, she began running through the forest, in hopes of meeting some of her friends ; but she only met with another robber. She was afraid he would kill her and the little prince, because they had nothing to give him. Margaret then fell upon her knees, and owned she was the queen, and begged the robber to protect his king's

Escape of Queen Margaret.

son. The robber was surprised, indeed, to see the queen and prince by themselves, half-starved, and weary with running in that wild place. But he was a good-natured man, and took them under his care; he got them some food, and took them to a cottage to rest; after which he contrived to take them safely to the seaside, where they got on board ship and went to Flanders.

Now that King Henry was safe in the Tower of London, and Queen Margaret was gone abroad, everybody in England hoped there would be an end to the civil wars, and King Edward of York married a beautiful lady called Elizabeth Woodville, and he had many children, and there was nothing but feasting and rejoicing.

But the king had two brothers, George Duke of Clarence, who was rather foolish, and Richard, who was young, brave, and clever, but ambitious and very passionate. It is said that he was nicknamed Crookback because of a deformity of one of his shoulders, but much that has been said about and against him may not have been true. The Duke of Clarence had married a daughter of the Earl of Warwick, who had been very useful to the Yorkists. But he was vexed with the king for marrying without asking his advice, so he determined to begin the civil war again.

This Earl of Warwick was a very brave man, but he was changeable; at one time he fought for Edward of York, at another for Margaret and Henry of Lancaster; so, as he chose to call first one of them king, and then the other, he was nicknamed the King-maker. Once Warwick forced King Edward to flee from England, and put Henry on the throne again. But Edward came back, and Warwick was killed in a battle at Barnet, near London, and poor Henry was sent back to the Tower.

About three weeks after that battle of Barnet there was another at Tewkesbury, where Edward of York took Queen Margaret prisoner and her son Edward was killed, though it may be that he was murdered after the battle. The truth about that is not known.

That miserable queen was sent to prison in the Tower immediately afterwards, where her poor husband was a prisoner. But a very few days after the battle of Tewkesbury, Henry was found dead in his prison, and he, too, was most likely murdered. The King of France paid Edward a large sum of money to set Queen Margaret free.

Now, all Edward of York's enemies being either dead or overcome, he feasted and enjoyed himself. His foolish brother, the Duke of Clarence, quarrelled with the queen and her relations, and also with the Duke of Gloucester. So Edward had Clarence sent to the Tower, where he was put to death. Many people thought that the Duke of Gloucester murdered King Henry the Sixth, and caused the Duke of Clarence to be drowned in a cask of Malmsey wine ; but I am not sure of any of this, for the many enemies of Richard, in their hatred of him after his death, made up many tales against him. There was great bitterness in England during those unhappy days.

In the springtime of 1483, King Edward the Fourth died, and left two little sons and five daughters.

I can say very little good of him, except that he was brave and handsome, and good-humoured in company ; but then he was cruel and revengeful ; and, when the wars were over he loved his own pleasure and amusement too well to do anything good or useful for the people, and he did them much wrong.

CHAPTER XXXIV

EDWARD V.—ONLY TEN WEEKS OF 1483

When Edward the Fourth died, his son Edward, Prince of Wales, was only thirteen years old ; and his younger son, Richard, Duke of York, only ten.

The Prince of Wales was with some of his relations at Ludlow, and the little duke with his mother in London.

Their guardian was their uncle, Richard, Duke of Gloucester, whose ambitious and passionate nature you read about in the last chapter.

Now the Duke of Gloucester wished to be King himself ; but there were several noblemen who determined to try to prevent his depriving his little nephew of the kingdom ; and when the boy was brought to London, and lodged in the palace in the Tower, to keep him safe, as his uncle said, they tried to watch over him, and prevent any wrong from being done to him. But Richard of Gloucester was too cunning for them. He contrived, in the first place, to get the little Duke of York out of his mother's hands, and to lodge him in the Tower, as well as his brother. He next declared that he wanted to talk with the little king's friends about the proper day for setting the crown on his head, and letting the people see him as their king. So the lords who wished well to the young princes all came to the Tower, and were sitting together waiting for the Duke of Gloucester.

At last he came, and said, very angrily, that he had found out several persons who were making plans to put him to death, and had bribed some persons to poison him ; and then, turning to Lord Hastings, who was one of young Edward's best friends, asked him fiercely what the persons deserved who had done so ? " They deserve severe punishment," said Lord Hastings, " IF they have done so."—" IF ! dost thou answer me with IFS ? " roared out Gloucester ; " by St. Paul, I will not dine till thy head is off ! "

The moment he had said this he struck his hand upon the table, and some soldiers came into the room. He made a sign to them to take away Lord Hastings, and they took him directly to the court before the windows. There they laid him down with his neck on a log of wood, and cut off his head, and the cruel Gloucester went to his dinner.

After this, nobody was surprised to hear that Richard had put to death several more of the king's friends ; and that the next thing he did was to get the people to make him king, and to say that the young prince was not fit to be a king.

After this, he ordered both the little princes to be murdered in the Tower ; and this is how it was done according to the popular belief, though you must remember that nobody can be sure of the truth of it.

The governor of the Tower at that time was Sir Robert Brackenbury, and Richard found that he was so honest, that while he was there he would not let anybody hurt the little princes, so that he sent away Brackenbury upon some business that was to take him two or three days, and gave the keys to a wicked servant of his own to keep till Brackenbury came back. The bad man's name was Tyrrell ; and he had no sooner got the charge of the little king and his brother, than he sent for two persons more wicked even than himself, and promised them a great deal of money, if they would go into the children's room while they were asleep and murder them.

These two men's names were Dighton and Forrest. They went into the room where the princes were both on the same bed. Their little arms were round each other's necks, and their little cheeks close together. Then the wicked murderers

Death of the little Princes in the Tower.

took some cushions, and laid them over the poor children as they lay asleep, and smothered them.

Then they took them on their shoulders, and carried them to a little back-staircase, near their room in the Tower, and buried them in a great hole under the stairs, and threw a heap of stones over them ; and a long time afterwards, some workmen, who were employed to repair that part of the Tower, found bones in that place which might have been theirs.

And this was the end of our little King Edward the Fifth, and his brother of York. It is said that the nursery tale of the Babes in the Wood and their wicked uncle was based upon the sad story of those young princes.

You will read something about their sister Elizabeth very soon.

CHAPTER XXXV

RICHARD III.—1483 TO 1485

Richard, Duke of Gloucester, had got himself made king, as I told you, before his young nephews in the Tower were murdered. The people were told that the young princes had died suddenly.

He tried to make the people forget the wicked way in which he came to be king by making some good laws ; but he could not succeed. The English could not love him, and Richard had but a short and troublesome reign.

The first vexation he had was caused by a cousin of his, the Duke of Buckingham, who was quite as bad a man as himself, and had helped him to become king in return for certain promises. But Richard did not keep those promises. So the Duke got an army together, and hoped by beginning a civil war to punish Richard ; but he was taken prisoner, and Richard treated him as he had done Lord Hastings, that is, he cut off his head directly.

There was another cousin of Richard's, and a much better man, about whom I must tell you a great deal more. His name was Henry Tudor, Earl of Richmond. Now his father, Edmund Tudor, Earl of Richmond, was related to the old princes of Wales, who you must remember were Britons, and his mother, the Countess of Richmond, was a lady of the family of Lancaster, or the Red Rose. Richard the Third hated the Earl of Richmond, because he knew that many people thought Henry ought to be king, and he did everything he could to injure him and his family. But Richmond himself was abroad, where Richard could not hurt him.

But after a little while Richmond wrote to his friends in England, that, if they would be ready to help him when he came, he would bring with him from abroad money and men, and then England might get rid of King Richard of the White Rose, and take him instead for their king.

The best gentlemen in England immediately got ready to receive Richmond ; all the relations of the persons Richard had put to death were glad to join with him to punish that bad man. The people in Wales were delighted to think of having one belonging to their ancient princes to be their king, and, not long after Richmond had landed at Milford Haven, he found several thousand men ready to follow him.

Richard, who was brave, although he was cruel, got ready an army also to fight Richmond, and he met him at a place called Bosworth, in Leicestershire, where they fought a great battle.

I have read that King Richard, when he was lying in his tent the night before the battle, could not help thinking of all the cruel things he had done. Besides those he had killed in battle, he remembered the young prince Edward of Lancaster, and others, and poor Henry the Sixth, who had been murdered in prison, and his own brother Clarence. Then he began to think of Lord Hastings, and all his friends, six or seven, I think, whom he had beheaded, and his little nephews, who were smothered in the Tower, and his cousin Buckingham, and, last of all, his wife, Queen Anne.

And so when he got up in the morning he was tired and unhappy, and did not fight so well as he might have done.

However that might be, he did fight very bravely and was

killed in the battle of Bosworth Field. His crown was found upon the field of battle, and Lord Stanley, who had deserted from Richard in the fighting, put it upon the Earl of Richmond's head, upon which the whole army shouted "Long live King Henry the Seventh!" and so from that day the British prince, Henry Tudor, Earl of Richmond, and heir of Lancaster, was King of England.

CHAPTER XXXVI

HENRY VII.—1485 TO 1509

When the Earl of Richmond was made king, and was called Henry the Seventh, many persons began to be afraid that the wars of the Roses would begin again. But Henry was a wise man, and he had made friends of the party of York, by promising to marry his cousin Elizabeth, the sister of the little princes who were smothered in the Tower. So, as soon as he was crowned himself, and the people had owned him for their king, he married Elizabeth ; and as Henry was King of the Red Rose party, and she was Queen of the White Rose party, the people agreed better than they had done for more than thirty years, and England began to be quiet and happy.

However, there were two disturbances in the beginning of Henry's reign that I must tell you of. There was a good-looking young man, called Lambert Simnel, that some people thought was very like the Earl of Warwick, a son of that Duke of Clarence who was killed in the Tower ; and some persons, who wished to annoy Henry the Seventh, persuaded Lambert to say he was Warwick, and that he had run away from the Tower, and had hidden himself till after his uncle Richard's death ; but that now, as Richard and his little cousins were all dead, he had a right to be king. Some few Englishmen joined him, and a good many Irish. But in a battle at Stoke, in the North of England, they were all driven away, and Lambert was taken prisoner.

The king, who knew the poor young man had been forced to do what he did by other people, did not send him to prison, but made him a turnspit in his kitchen ; and, as he behaved very well there, he afterwards gave him the care of his hawks.

Marriage of King Henry VII. and Elizabeth of York.

The second disturbance was of more consequence. A young man, called Perkin Warbeck, was taught by one of King Henry's enemies, the Duchess of Burgundy, to call himself Richard Duke of York.

He said that he was the brother to the little king who was killed in the Tower, and that Dighton and Forrest could not bear to kill them both, and that he had hidden himself till he could get to the duchess, who, as he said, was his aunt.

Now King Henry knew this story was not true, yet it vexed him very much. For Perkin Warbeck prevailed on several noblemen in Ireland to take his part, and he went to Scotland, and got the king to believe him, and to let him marry a beautiful young lady, named Catharine Gordon, the king's own cousin, and to march into England with an army, where he did a great deal of mischief before King Henry's army could drive him away. Then Perkin sailed to Cornwall, and collected a small army ; but after doing just enough mischief to make everybody fear him and his people, he was taken prisoner by King Henry, who kept him some time in the Tower : at last he was hanged at Tyburn, and nobody was sorry for him but his poor wife Lady Catharine.

King Henry sent for that unfortunate lady, and took her to the queen, who treated her very kindly, and made her live with her, and did all she could to make her happy again.

England was quiet for the rest of King Henry's reign ; and Wales, which had been ill-treated by the Kings of England ever since Edward the First conquered it, was better treated by Henry.

As there was no fighting, the young men began to try to improve themselves in learning. Some years before that time, some clever men in Germany had found out how to print books instead of copying them in writing, so there were a great many more books, and more people could learn to read. The young men in Cambridge and Oxford began to read the good books that had been forgotten in the wars of the Roses, and they were ashamed to find that there were not half a dozen men in England who knew anything at all about Greek. I think one of those few was Grocyn, a teacher at Oxford.

But the English had soon a very good Greek teacher. A young man born at Canterbury, called Thomas Linacre, after learning all he could at the school in his own town, and at Oxford, went to travel in Italy, where the most learned men in the world lived at that time. These learned men soon found out that Thomas Linacre was very clever indeed, and so they helped him to learn everything that he desired, for the sake of improving his own country when he came back. He studied everything so carefully, that on his return to Oxford the greatest and wisest men went to him to be taught Greek, besides many other things he had learned in his travels. He was chosen to be tutor to the king's eldest son, Prince Arthur, and he was afterwards tutor to some of the next king's children. He was the greatest physician in England, and before he died he founded the same College of Physicians that we have now.

In the next chapter we shall have a great deal to read about several of Linacre's scholars ; but I tell you about him now that you may know that it was in this king's time that the gentlemen of England began to think of reading and studying, instead of doing nothing but hunt and fight.

About this time, sailors from Europe first found their way to America. Christopher Columbus went from Spain, Americo Vespucci from Italy, and Sebastian Cabot from England. They all arrived safe at the other side of the wide ocean, and then it was first known for certain that there was such a place as America. How surprised all their friends must have been, when they came home, and told of the strange things they had seen ! The trees and the flowers were different from ours. The birds were larger, and had more beautiful feathers ; the butterflies had gayer colours than we had ever seen. Then they brought home turkeys, which they found in the woods, and potatoes, which they had eaten for the first time, to plant in our fields and gardens. But I should fill a whole book if I tried to tell you of all the things that were brought from the new countries found out in Henry the Seventh's time.

We must now speak of the king himself. His wife, Elizabeth of York, was dead. She had four children, Arthur and Henry, Mary and Margaret. Mary became Queen of France, and Margaret Queen of Scotland. Arthur, who was the eldest, was good and clever, but sickly, and he died before his father ; so Henry was the next king.

Henry the Seventh was a wise man, and a severe king. His greatest fault was loving money, so that he took unjust ways to get it from his subjects. He was very unwilling to spend anything upon himself or other people. But yet he laid out a great deal of money in building a great palace at Richmond, and in adding a beautiful chapel to Westminster Abbey, and in other fine buildings. He sent to Italy for painters and sculptors, to make pictures and statues ; and he was fond of encouraging learning and trade.

But though he did many good and useful things, nobody loved him, for he had a cold and selfish nature ; and when he died very few persons were sorry for him.

CHAPTER XXXVII

HENRY VIII.—1509 TO 1547

I have so many things to tell you about Henry the Eighth, that I dare say I shall fill three chapters.

When he first became king, everybody liked him. He was handsome, and generous, and good-humoured. Besides all that, he was clever, and learned ; he liked the company of wise men, and treated them kindly. One of his great amusements after dinner was to invite the greatest scholars and the cleverest men, such as clergymen, lawyers, physicians, and painters, to go and talk with him. And so he learned a great deal from hearing what they said.

But as Henry grew older, I am sorry to say that he changed, and became cruel and hard-hearted, as you will read by and by.

The wise old king, Henry the Seventh, had been very careful to keep peace with the French and the Scots all his life, but the young king liked the thoughts of gaining a little glory by fighting ; so soon after he became king, he had a war with France, and another with Scotland.

The war with Scotland ended sadly for the Scots. The English army was commanded by a brave nobleman, named the Earl of Surrey, and he had with him several lords and knights. The Scottish army was almost all made up of the boldest and best men in Scotland, with their own king, James the Fourth, to command them. The two armies met at a place called Flodden Field. They fought all day ; sometimes one side got the better and sometimes the other; so when night came, nobody knew which had beaten the other. But in the morning the Scots found that they had lost their king, whom they all loved very much, and that with him the best and bravest of the Scottish nobles had been killed.

After this there was peace between Scotland and England.

As to King Henry's war in France, it did not last long. I told you Henry was young, and wished for the kind of glory that princes gain by fighting. But he forgot that, besides glory, there must be a great deal of fatigue and suffering; so, after one battle, he was persuaded to make peace. That one battle was called the Battle of the Spurs, because the French made more use of their spurs, to make their horses run away, than of their swords to fight with.

Not long after this battle, the old French king died. The new king was called Francis the First. He was almost as young as Henry the Eighth. He was handsome, too, and very fond of gaiety, and dancing, and riding, and feasting, and playing at fighting, which was called jousting. So the two young kings agreed that they would meet together, and have some merry days. And so they did.

They met near a place called Ardres, in France. The richest noblemen, both of France and England, and their wives and daughters, were there. The tents they feasted in were made of silk, with gold flowers; their dresses were covered over with gold and jewels; even their very horses were dressed up with silk and golden fringes; and there was feasting, and dancing, and jousting, and music every day.

The two kings amused themselves with dancing, and all sorts of games, till at last they found it was time to go home, and mind the affairs of their own kingdoms.

This meeting was called THE FIELD OF THE CLOTH OF GOLD,

because there was so much gold in the dresses and tents, and the ornaments used by the kings and their lords and ladies.

Besides the two kings who were at the Field of the Cloth of Gold, there was a great man there, whom you must know

Henry VIII. embarking for France.

something about. His name was Wolsey. He was a clergyman, and in the time of King Henry the Seventh he was known to be very clever indeed. But Henry the Eighth first made him a bishop, and then the Pope (who you know is the Bishop of Rome) gave him the rank of Cardinal.

In those days a cardinal was thought to be almost as great a man as a king. He dressed in long fine silk robes, trimmed with fur, and when he went out he wore a scarlet hat with a broad brim and fine red cords and tassels.

This Cardinal Wolsey was very clever, as I told you, and very learned ; he was one of the scholars at Oxford when Thomas Linacre taught Greek there ; and with a part of the great riches that he got from the king he built the great college, called Christ Church, at Oxford, and a school at Ipswich, the town where he was born. He also built the great palace of Hampton Court, and made a present of it to the king. And these you know were all useful things.

But Cardinal Wolsey was proud towards the nobles, and had to tax the people heavily to pay for the king's wars ; so he was greatly disliked. And some persons told the king that the cardinal spoke ill of him, and that he boasted of being richer and more powerful than the king. So Henry, who was passionate, ordered all his riches to be taken away from him, and sent for him to London, where I am almost sure he intended to order his head to be cut off. But the cardinal fell ill and died on the road. His last words were—" If I had served God as diligently as I have served the king, He would not have given me over in my grey hairs."

Now I must end this chapter. In the next I shall tell you about King Henry's six wives.

CHAPTER XXXVIII

HENRY VIII.—(*continued*)

Henry the Eighth's first wife was Catherine of Aragon. She was a princess from Spain, who came to England to be married to Prince Arthur, King Henry's elder brother. But as you read in the chapter before the last, Prince Arthur died when he was very young ; and Catherine was married to Henry.

They had only one daughter, the Princess Mary, who came to be Queen of England, as you will read. Now, though Henry was very fond of his wife for a great many years, he grew tired of her at last, and wished very much to marry a beautiful young lady who had come to the Court.

He determined to get some of those people who are always willing to do as their king pleases, instead of being honest and doing only what is right, to find out some excuses for sending away good Queen Catherine, for indeed she was very good, and loved the king dearly. So at last they found some, which you could not understand if I told you ; and they divorced Queen Catherine, that is, they sent her away from the king, and said he might marry anybody else that he pleased.

The good queen lived about three years afterwards, sometimes at Ampthill, sometimes at other country places, and died at Kimbolton.

The second wife of Henry was the beautiful young lady, Anne Boleyn, whose daughter Elizabeth became Queen of England after her sister Mary. But now King Henry, who

Wolsey entering Leicester Abbey.

had found out that he could make excuses for sending away one wife, began to wish for another change.

I told you Anne Boleyn was young and beautiful. She was also clever and pleasant although proud and high-spirited. But the king and some of his friends were told that she had done several bad things ; and, as Henry had become very cruel as well as changeable, he ordered poor Anne's head to be cut off.

On the day she was to suffer death she sent to beg the king to be kind to her little daughter Elizabeth. She said to the last moment that she was innocent ; she prayed God to bless the king and the people, and then she knelt down, and her head was cut off.

I ought to have told you, that, before she was brought out of her room to be beheaded, she said to the gentleman who went to call her, " I hear the executioner is very skilful ; my neck is very small ; " and she put her hands round it and smiled, and made ready to go to die.

The wicked king married another very pretty young woman the very next day. Her name was Jane Seymour, and she had a son, who was afterwards King Edward the Sixth. She died twelve days after the little prince was born, and Henry was very grieved over her death, though very glad that he now had a son to succeed him.

The king's fourth wife was found for him by his minister, Thomas Cromwell. She was the Princess Anne of Cleves, a German lady. But Henry took a dislike to her looks, so he put her away as he did Queen Catherine, and gave her a house to live in, and a good deal of money to spend, and thought no more about her except as a friend.

Next he married the Lady Catherine Howard ; but a very few months afterwards he accused her of some bad actions ;

and he had her beheaded. So he had put away two of his wives, he had cut off the heads of two others, and only one had died a natural death.

Yet he found a lady, named Catherine Parr, who was a widow ; and she married him very willingly, for she was ready to run the risk for the sake of being a queen. She was clever, and contrived to keep the passionate and cruel king in good humour till he died, when I dare say she was not sorry to find herself alive and safe, for he had once intended to put her to death as he had done Anne Boleyn and Catherine Howard.

Now we will end this chapter about Henry's wives. You will find that as he grew older he grew more and more passionate and cruel ; and in what I have to tell you about some other parts of his reign, in the next chapter, you will see that he grew wicked in many ways.

CHAPTER XXXIX

HENRY VIII.—(*continued*)

In several parts of our history we have read of the Pope, that is, the Bishop of Rome. When Thomas Becket was murdered in the reign of Henry the Second, I told you it was done after a quarrel between the king and Thomas, because Thomas wanted the Pope to have the power to punish clergymen in England, or to let them go without punishment, when they did wrong, without caring at all what the law of the country might be.

Now more than three hundred years had passed, and the Popes still had great power. And a great many new kinds of clergymen, especially the FRIARS, had begun to go about the country, doing nothing themselves, and pretending that the people ought to give them meat, and drink, and lodging, because they could read and say prayers. Besides that, they used to pretend to cure diseases, by making people kiss old bones, or bits of rag, and other trash, which they said had once belonged to some holy person or another, which was as wicked as it was foolish. It was wicked to tell such lies or else it was through ignorance. It was foolish, because the cures that God has appointed for diseases are only to be learned by care and patience, and have nothing to do with such things as old bones and rags.

However, almost everybody believed these things for a long time. But at last, people began to read more books, as I told you in the chapter about Henry the Seventh ; and they learned how foolish it was to believe all the friars had said.

One of the first books they began to read was the Bible, in which they found the commands of God ; and they saw that all men ought to obey the laws of the countries they live in. And they found that clergymen might marry, and that, though they ought to be paid for teaching the people, they had no business to live idly.

It was not only in England that the people began to think of these things, but in other countries, especially in Germany, where a learned man, named Martin Luther, was the first who dared to tell the clergymen how ill he thought they behaved, and to try to persuade all kings and princes to forbid the Pope's messengers and priests to meddle with the proper laws of the country. There were many other things he found fault with very justly, which I cannot tell you now, as we must speak of what was done in England.

You have not forgotten that I told you that men, and some women as well, began to study a great deal in the reign of Henry the Seventh, and I promised to tell you something about Thomas Linacre's scholars.

One of these was a gentleman of Rotterdam, in Holland, who came to England on purpose to learn Greek. His name was Erasmus, and he was famous for writing better Latin than anybody had done since the time of the old Romans.

Another was Sir Thomas More, who was Lord Chancellor of England during part of Henry the Eighth's reign ; he was very learned and wise, and, besides that, good-humoured and cheerful.

Erasmus and Sir Thomas More were great friends, especially when Sir Thomas was young ; and they used to write pleasant letters and books, to show how wrong those persons were who believed in the foolish stories told by the friars, and how wicked many of the clergymen were, who lived idle lives, and passed their time in eating and drinking, and in doing many bad things, instead of teaching the people, as it was their duty to do.

Besides these two great friends, there were several others, especially Tonstall and Latimer, who both were taught by Linacre, and are remembered to our time for being learned and good.

By degrees, the English heard all that Martin Luther said in Germany about the Pope and his friars, and the bad part of the clergymen; and many disputes arose among the people. Some said that we had no business to obey the Pope at all in anything, and that many of the things the clergymen of Rome taught were wicked and false, and that God would punish those who believed them, now that they could read the Bible, and learn for themselves what was right.

Others said that those things were not false, and that we ought to believe them; and as to the Pope, we ought to obey him in everything about our churches and our prayers, and the way of worshipping God.

But the thing that made the people who took the opposite side in the dispute most angry, was the quantity of land and money that the clergymen had persuaded different people to give them. Those who were against the Pope said that the clergymen had deceived the people and had pretended that they could prevail upon God to forgive their worst sins, if they would only give their lands and money to the churches and convents, that the monks and friars might live in idleness.

The others, who were for the Pope, pretended that clergy-men were better and wiser than others, and therefore they ought to live in comfort, and grandeur, and leisure, and to have more power and money than other men.

Now I believe the truth is, that in those days the clergymen were a great deal too rich and powerful, and that they oppressed the people in every country, and that they tried to keep them from learning to read, that they might not find out the truth from the Bible and other good books.

However, in England there were a great many good men on both sides.

At first, the king took the part of the Pope, and, as he was very fond of showing his learning, he wrote a book to defend him against Martin Luther ; in return for which the Pope called Henry the DEFENDER OF THE FAITH.

But soon afterwards King Henry began to change his mind. He thought the English clergymen would be better governed if the King of England were at their head instead of the Pope. Then he thought that, if all the convents were pulled down, and the monks and nuns made to live like other people, instead of idly, without doing anything, he might take their lands and money and give to his servants, or spend himself, just as he liked.

As soon as Henry thought of these things, he set about doing what he wished. He would not listen even to the old men and women, who had lived in the convents till they were too old to work ; he turned them all out. He would not listen to some good advice about leaving a few convents for those who took care of the strangers and sick people, but, like a cruel and passionate man as he was, he turned them all out : many of them actually died of hunger and distress, and many more ended their lives as beggars.

Yet, although Henry was so cruel to the monks and priests, he would not allow the people to change many of the things that the followers of the Pope were most to blame for. He was glad enough to be master, or, as he called it, SUPREME HEAD of the English church and clergy, and to take the lands and money from the convents and abbeys. But he would not let everybody read the Bible, and would insist upon their worshipping God as he pleased, not in the way they believed to be right.

I have already told you that many very good men wished a great many changes to be made in the manner of worship, in teaching the people, and letting them read ; besides taking some of the lands and money of the convents, and forcing the clergymen to use the rest of their riches properly. Besides, they wished the clergymen to be allowed to marry.

The chief persons who wished for these changes were— Cranmer, Archbishop of Canterbury ; Latimer, Bishop of Worcester ; Shaxton, Bishop of Salisbury ; all learned men ; and they had most of the gentlemen and many of the people with them.

Those who followed after these wise men were called Protestants.

But there were many great and good men who thought that the clergymen might alter some small things for the better, but they would not consent to pulling down the convents, nor taking their lands and money, nor to changing the way of worshipping God, nor to the king's being at the head of the Church of England, instead of the Pope. These men were called Papists.

At the head of them were—Sir Thomas More ; Tonstall, Bishop of Durham ; Warham, Archbishop of Canterbury ; and most of the lords in the kingdom.

Now King Henry, although he chose to change the way of worship a little, and liked very well, as I said before, to get

all the lands and money into his hands, still wanted to go on
with some of the worst customs of the old clergymen, and,
according to his cruel temper, he made some very hard laws,
and threatened to burn people alive who would not believe
what he believed, and worship God in the way he chose.

Many people, who could hardly understand what the king
meant, were really burnt alive, according to that wicked law :
but the thing that showed Henry's badness more than any
other, was his ordering Sir Thomas More's head to be cut off,
because he would not do as the king wished, nor say what he
did not think was true. But I will write a chapter about that
good man on purpose, after we have done with this wicked
King Henry.

Besides putting Sir Thomas More to death, the king cut
off the heads of Bishop Fisher, the Marquis of Exeter, Lord
Montague, Sir Edward Nevil, and, most shocking of all, the
head of an old lady with grey hairs, named Margaret Plantagenet, only because her son, Reginald Pole, afterwards
called Cardinal Pole, would not come to England when
Henry invited him.

I dare say you are tired of reading of so much wickedness.
I am sure I am tired of writing it, and I will only mention one
thing more. A few days before Henry died he ordered the
Earl of Surrey's head to be cut off.

This Earl of Surrey was the most polite and pleasant, and
clever young gentleman in England. But Henry was afraid
that he would give trouble to his little son after his death.
He was also going to cut off the head of Surrey's father, the
old Duke of Norfolk, but the king died the night before that
was to have been done, and so the Duke was saved. I do not
believe that there were many in England who could be sorry
when Henry died.

CHAPTER XL

THE STORY OF SIR THOMAS MORE

Well, my dear little Arthur, that is nearly all that I have to say about King Henry the Eighth, and I am going to keep my promise, and write a little chapter about Sir Thomas More.

We read in the chapter about Henry the Seventh, that in his reign the young gentlemen of England began to study and read, and even to write books, instead of spending all their time in fighting or hunting. And I told you that Thomas Linacre, the great physician, taught a great many gentlemen at Oxford to read and write Greek, and that Sir Thomas More was one of his scholars.

Sir Thomas More's father wished him to be a lawyer, and, though he did not like it himself, he left his other learning and studied law to please his father, and he became a great lawyer.

He was handsome and good-natured, very cheerful, and fond of laughing. He had a pleasant voice, and it is said that he was the first Englishman who could be called an orator, that is, a man who can speak well before a great number of others, and either teach them or persuade them to think or do as he wishes.

But what you will like best to hear is, how good he was to his little son and his daughters : he used to laugh with them and talk with them, and as he had a pretty garden round his house at Chelsea, he used to walk and play with them there.

Besides this, he was so kind to them, that he had the best

masters in England to teach them different languages, and music ; and they used to have very pleasant concerts, when his wife and daughters used to play on different instruments, and sing to him. He was very fond of painting, and had the famous painter, Hans Holbein, in his house a long time.

Sometimes he and his children read pleasant books together, and he was particularly careful to instruct his little girls, and they read and wrote Latin very well, besides being very good workwomen with their needles, and understanding how to take care of a house.

You may think what a happy family this was, and how much all the children and the parents loved one another. All the best men that were then alive used to come now and then and see Sir Thomas More and his family. There was the famous Erasmus, whom I mentioned before ; and Bishop Tonstall, who often contrived to save people from the cruel Henry, when he had ordered them to be burnt ; and Dean Colet, who began that good school at St. Paul's, in London, for boys whose parents were too poor to have them properly taught. You may think how happy Sir Thomas More was at Chelsea, loving his wife and children, who were all good, and most of them clever, and seeing his good and wise friends every day.

But you know that God gives men duties to do for the country they live in as well as for themselves ; and as Sir Thomas More was a lawyer, he was obliged to attend to his business, and when he became a judge, it took up so much of his time that he could not be so much at his house at Chelsea as he wished. It was still worse when Henry the Eighth made him Lord Chancellor of England, and required most of his spare time to talk with him, instead of letting him go home.

For some time King Henry liked him very much, and

everybody was in hopes that he might make the king a better man.

But Henry was too bad and too wilful to take advice when it went against his hopes and wishes. The first dislike he showed to Sir Thomas More was because that honest man did not wish him to send away his good wife, Catherine of Aragon, and marry another woman while she was alive. Afterwards he was angry with him because he would not leave off thinking that the Pope was head of the Christian Church, and say what Henry pleased, though he tried every means to persuade him to do so.

At last the king sent him to prison on that account, and kept him there a whole year, and sent all sorts of people to him, to try and get him to say the king was in the right, whatever he might say or do, and particularly that it was right for him to be called the Supreme Head of the Church of England.

But More would not tell a lie. He knew his duty to God required him to speak the truth ; and as he thought the king wrong, he said so boldly. This so enraged the cruel tyrant, that he determined to put him to death ; but he made believe to be sorry, and said he should have a fair trial, and sent for him out of prison, and made a number of noblemen and gentlemen ask him the same things over again that he had been asked in prison before. And as he still gave the same answers, the king ordered his head to be cut off.

In all the whole year he had been in prison he had only been allowed to see his wife once ; and his eldest daughter Margaret, who was married to a Mr. Roper, once also. The cruel king now ordered that he should be kept in prison, without seeing any of his family again before his death ; but Margaret Roper waited in the street, and knelt down near where he must pass, that he might give her his blessing. Then she determined to try to kiss her own dear father before he died ; so, without minding the soldiers who were carrying him to prison, or the crowd which were standing round, she ran past them all and caught her father in her arms, and kissed him over and over again, and cried so bitterly that even the soldiers could not help crying too.

The only thing More begged of the king on the day he was beheaded was, that his dear daughter might be allowed to go to his funeral ; and he felt happy when they told him all his family might go.

After Sir Thomas More's head was cut off, the cruel king ordered it to be stuck upon a pole on London bridge ; but Margaret Roper soon contrived to get it down. She kept it carefully till she died, and then it was buried with her.

As long as there are any good people in the world, Sir Thomas More and his daughter will be loved whenever their names are heard.

CHAPTER XLI

EDWARD VI.—1547 TO 1553

When King Henry the Eighth died, his only son, who was but nine years old, was made king under the name of Edward the Sixth.

Of course the little prince could not do much of a king's proper business himself ; but his guardians, and especially his mother's brother, managed the kingdom tolerably well for him at first.

The little boy was very gentle and fond of learning. He was serious and clever too : he wrote down in a book every day what he had been about, and seemed to wish to do what was right ; so the people thought they might have a really good king.

I told you, when I mentioned the alteration in religion in Henry the Eighth's reign, that though nearly all the nobles continued Papists, yet many of the gentlemen and the people were Protestants. Now King Edward's uncles and teachers were Protestants, and they taught the young king to be one also, and laws were made by which all the people in England were ordered to be Protestants too.

The Bible was allowed to be read by everybody who chose it, in English, and the clergymen were ordered to say the prayers in English instead of Latin, which very few could understand. The king was declared to be the head of the Church ; clergymen were allowed to marry ; and those persons whom Henry the Eighth had put in prison were set free.

These things were not only good for the people then, but they have been of use ever since. As the English clergymen, and schools, and colleges, have had no foreign Pope to interfere with them, they have been able to teach such things as are good and useful to England. Clergymen who are married, and have families living in the country among the farmers and cottagers, may set good examples and teach useful things, by the help of their wives and children, which the clergy who were not married could never do.

And as for reading the Bible, and saying prayers in English, it must be better for us all to learn our duties, and speak of our wants to God, in the language we understand best.

For these reasons the reign of Edward the Sixth is always reckoned a good one for England.

There were, however, some very wrong things done in it, and some unhappy ones, owing to the king's being so young.

I told you he was only nine years old when he came to be king. Those in whose care his father had placed him and the kingdom, allowed one of the king's uncles, the Duke of Somerset, to become his chief guardian and adviser, and he is always called the Lord Protector Somerset.

A quarrel which Henry the Eighth had begun with Scotland was carried on by Somerset, who went himself to Scotland with an army, and beat the Scots at the battle of Pinkie; but the war did no good, and was not even honourable to England. Somerset offered to make peace if the Scottish lords would allow their young Queen Mary to marry our young King Edward, when the children were old enough, and then England and Scotland might have been one kingdom from that time.

I should tell you that the last king of Scotland, James the Fifth, was dead, and that his widow was a French lady, who ruled the kingdom, with the help of the Scottish nobles, for her little daughter, who was five years old. She and the nobles at that time were Papists, and would not allow Mary to marry the Protestant King Edward of England, but sent her to France, where she married a French prince, and was Queen of France for a little while.

When the Protector Somerset came back from Scotland, the great lords at first seemed glad to see him ; but by degrees they made the young king think very ill of him. Besides, many hated Somerset for his pride. He pulled down churches and bishops' palaces, to make room for his own palace in the Strand. The great building that now stands in the same place is still called Somerset House.

I am sorry to tell you that one of the Protector's enemies was his own brother, Lord Seymour of Sudely, a brave but unruly man, who was the High Admiral of England.

Now the Admiral wished to be the king's guardian instead of Somerset ; and he was trying to do this by force. So he was seized and tried ; and his own brother, the Protector, signed the order for him to be beheaded.

Somerset did this to save his own life ; but soon after this his enemies grew too strong for him, and Lord Warwick, who had become the chief ruler, got the king to sign an order to behead Somerset.

Although he was a king, the poor boy must have been very unhappy. He had been persuaded to order his own two uncles to be beheaded ; and although he had two sisters, he and they did not live together and he really knew little about them.

The eldest was the daughter of Henry the Eighth's first wife, Catherine of Aragon. She was twenty-one years older than the king, and she was a Papist, and earnest and narrow in her religion.

The king's second sister was the daughter of poor Queen Anne Boleyn. Her name was Elizabeth; she was a Protestant, and was only four years older than her brother, who loved her, and used to call her his " sweet sister Temperance."

The Protector Somerset accusing his Brother before King Edward VI.

He had one cousin, whom he saw often, and who was beautiful and good, and loved learning; her name was Lady Jane Grey. I shall have a good deal to tell you about her, and how she used to read and learn as well as the little king.

But I must now tell you what happened when the Protector was beheaded. Although he had offended the great lords, and they had persuaded the king that he deserved to die, the people loved him. He had always been kind to them, and the laws made while he was Protector were all good for England. On the day when his head was cut off on Tower-Hill—it was early in the morning—a great many people were collected to see him die. Suddenly one of the king's messengers rode up to the scaffold where Somerset stood ready for the executioner; the people hoped the king had sent a pardon for his uncle, and shouted out, " A pardon ! a pardon ! God save the king ! " But it was not true ; there was no pardon. Somerset was a little moved when the people shouted, but he soon became quite quiet. He spoke kindly and thankfully to some of his friends who were shedding tears near him, and then laid his head upon the block, and was beheaded.

After this time the Earl of Warwick managed the country for the king. But the poor young prince did not live long. Soon after his uncle's death he began to cough and look very ill, and everybody saw that he was likely to die.

Now the person who was to reign over England after Edward's death was his eldest sister, the Princess Mary, and as I told you, she was a Papist, or, as we now call it, a Roman Catholic.

The Earl of Warwick, who had been made Duke of Northumberland, had a son named Lord Guildford Dudley, who married the king's good and beautiful cousin, Lady Jane Grey. These young people were both Protestants, and Northumberland hoped that the people would like to have Lady Jane for their queen, in case the young king should die, better than the Roman Catholic Princess Mary ; and then he thought that, as he was the father of Jane's husband, he might rule the kingdom in her name, and get all the power for himself.

Poor King Edward now grew weaker and weaker : he was taken to Greenwich for change of air, and seemed at first a little better, so that the people, who really loved their gentle and sweet-tempered young king, began to hope he might live.

But Northumberland knew that Edward was dying, and he never left him, that he might persuade him to make a will, leaving the kingdom to his dear cousin, Lady Jane Grey, after his death.

This was very wrong, because the king is only placed at the head of the kingdom, to do justice and to exercise mercy. He cannot buy or sell the kingdom, or any part of it. He cannot change the owner of the smallest bit of land without the authority of the whole parliament, made up of the king himself, and the lords and gentlemen of the commons along with him. Of course, therefore, Northumberland was wrong, in persuading the young king to make such a will without the advice of parliament. You will read presently how Northumberland was punished.

Soon after this will was made poor Edward the Sixth died. He was not quite sixteen years old. He was so mild and gentle, that everybody pitied him. He took such pains to learn, and do what was right, that the people were in hopes of having a really good and wise king. But it pleased God that he should die. His last prayer as he lay a-dying was, " O Lord, save thy chosen people of England."

CHAPTER XLII

THE STORY OF LADY JANE GREY

Two days after King Edward died, Northumberland had Lady Jane Grey proclaimed, or publicly called queen, in London.

On the same day the Lady Mary's friends had her proclaimed at Norwich.

Some people would have liked Lady Jane best, first, because they believed their dear young King Edward had wished her to be queen; and next, because she was beautiful, virtuous, and wise, and, above all, a Protestant. But then they feared and hated her father-in-law, Northumberland. They remembered that he had persuaded King Edward to order the Protector Somerset to be beheaded. They knew that he was cruel, jealous, and revengeful; they thought that he only pretended to be a Protestant, and because he was such a bad man, they were afraid to let his son's wife be queen.

One by one all Northumberland's friends left him and joined the Princess Mary, who was the rightful queen; and after Lady Jane Grey had been called queen for ten days, she went to her private home at Sion House, a great deal happier than the day when they took her away to make her a queen.

It would have been well if Queen Mary had left her cousin there. But she was of a morose temper, and not content with sending Northumberland to prison in the Tower of London, for setting up her cousin as queen, she sent Lady Jane and her husband, Lord Guildford Dudley, also to the Tower.

But I must tell you more about Lady Jane Grey, and I will begin her story at the time when she was very young indeed.

As she was only a few months older than her cousin Edward the Sixth, they had the same teachers, and she was like him in gentleness, goodness, and kindness. Her masters found that she was still cleverer than the little king, and that she learned Latin and Greek too more readily than he did.

Lady Jane Grey refusing the Crown.

She knew French and Spanish, and Italian perfectly, and loved music and painting. She used to thank God that she had strict parents and a kind and gentle schoolmaster.

She was married when very young to Lord Guildford Dudley, only a few weeks before King Edward died; and she was very sorry when she found out that her husband wanted to be king.

When King Edward died, Lady Jane's father, the Duke of Suffolk, and her husband's father, the Duke of Northumberland, went to Lady Jane, and fell upon their knees before her, and offered her the crown of England, at the same time telling her that her cousin the king, whom she loved very much, was dead. On hearing this she fainted, and then refused the crown, saying, that while the ladies Mary and Elizabeth were alive, nobody else could have a right to it.

At last, however, though the two dukes could not prevail upon her to allow herself to be called Queen of England, her husband and her mother begged her so hard to be queen, that she consented.

I have already told you that she was only called queen for ten days, and that Queen Mary sent her and her husband to the Tower.

They were not allowed to see one another in their prison. However, as they were not beheaded immediately, people hoped that Mary would spare them. After she had kept them closely shut up for nearly eight months, a rebellion broke out and its leaders said they wanted to put Lady Jane again on the throne, so then the wretched queen ordered their heads to be cut off. Dudley was to be executed on Tower-Hill, in sight of all the people ; Lady Jane in a court within the Tower, with only a few persons round her.

When Lady Jane knew this, she had no wish to do anything but prepare for her own death next day. She wrote a letter to her father, to take leave of him, in which she said, " My guiltless blood may cry before the Lord, mercy to the innocent ! " She left her Greek Testament to her sister Catherine, with a Greek letter written on a blank leaf in it.

Early in the morning of the 12th day of February Lady Jane stood by the iron-barred window of her prison, and saw her dear husband led through the Tower gate to be beheaded. Not long afterwards she was praying near the same spot, and saw a common cart coming from the gate, and in it her husband's body, all covered with blood.

When she was taken from prison to be beheaded, she spoke kindly and gently to everybody near her. As Sir John Brydges, the keeper of the Tower, led her from her room to the scaffold, he asked her for a keepsake, and she gave him a little book, in which she had written three sentences, one in Greek, one in Latin, and one in English.

She spoke to the officers and servants before she was beheaded, saying that she had never intended to do wrong, that she only obeyed her parents in being queen, and that she trusted to be forgiven.

Her maidens then took off some part of her dress; she knelt down and laid her head upon the block, and her beautiful head was cut off before she was seventeen years old.

The people now were sorry they had allowed Mary to be queen, for they thought that if she could order these two good and innocent young people to be put to death, she would not spare anybody whom she might happen to hate. But only over religion was she really bitter or cruel, and during much of her early life she had been very unkindly treated, so that her mind was warped.

CHAPTER XLIII

MARY—1553 TO 1558

Mary, the daughter of Henry the Eighth, and of Catherine of Aragon, his first wife, was at Hunsdon when her brother died ; but instead of going directly to London to be made queen, she went first to Norwich, for fear of the Duke of Northumberland, and afterwards to London, as you read in the last chapter.

One of the very first things she did was to order the heads of the Duke of Northumberland and several other gentlemen to be cut off, for they had proved dangerous enemies to her. She then offended the people by forbidding them to say their public prayers or to read the Bible in English ; she ordered all the clergymen to send away their wives, and she determined to restore the Roman Catholic worship.

Many now began to be sorry that Mary was queen, and a number of people collected under the command of Sir Thomas Wyatt and the Duke of Suffolk, to try to drive Mary out, and release Lady Jane, for this was before she was put to death. At one time Mary was in great danger, but Wyatt's men fell away from him, and he was taken and put to death.

The queen, misled by her counsellors, was determined to be revenged on those who had been with Sir Thomas Wyatt. Besides beheading Lady Jane, as I have told you, she ordered the heads of the Duke of Suffolk and of many more gentlemen to be cut off, and stuck up the heads on poles all about the streets. She had fifty-two gentlemen hanged, all on the same day, and the people called the day Black Monday. She soon sent to fetch her sister Elizabeth from her house a Ashbridge, and on her coming to London sent her to the Tower. For two months Elizabeth was kept close in prison whilst her enemies strove hard to have her beheaded. At las her friends prevailed, and she was sent to live at Hatfield.

The next thing Mary did to offend the people of England was to marry the Spanish prince, who was soon after Philip the Second, King of Spain. He was as ill-tempered and a cruel as the queen, and encouraged her in hating the Pro testants, and in trying to make all the English people Roman Catholics again.

The queen's cousin, Cardinal Pole, was soon sent from Rome by the Pope. And one day Queen Mary and King Philip, with the nobles and commons, knelt before the Cardinal, and confessed the wickedness of England in casting off the power of the Pope. So the Cardinal forgave them and received England back to the Roman Church.

The persons who helped Mary most in her cruelty wer Gardiner, Bishop of Winchester, and Bishop Bonner. These two men were the most cruel I ever heard of, and determined to burn everybody who would not agree with the queen in her religion.

The first person Gardiner ordered to be burnt alive wa one of the clergymen belonging to the great church of St Paul in London; his name was Rogers. That good man would not do what he thought wrong towards God to pleas either Gardiner or the queen, so they sent him to the grea square called Smithfield, and there had him tied to a stake and a fire lighted all round him, so as to kill him. As he wa going along to be burnt, his wife and his ten little childre met him, and kissed him, and took leave of him, for Gardine would not let them go to him while he kept him in prison before his death.

The next was Dr. Hooper, Bishop of Gloucester. He died saying prayers, and preaching to the people round about him, and thanking God for giving him strength to speak the truth, and keep His commandments.

Altogether, there were nearly three hundred men and women burnt by Queen Mary's orders ; but I will only tell you the names of three more, for I hate to write about such very unhappy doings.

You remember I mentioned Bishop Latimer among the good men who were Protestants. He had come to be a very old man in Mary's reign ; but she would not spare him, but sent him with another bishop, a friend of his, as good and learned as himself, named Ridley, to Oxford, where they were burned together, only because they were Protestants.

At last Mary determined to order the death of the wise and good Archbishop Cranmer. He had always been very gentle and rather fearful, and he wrote to Mary, and tried by every means to get her to allow him to live. They made him hope to be spared if he would give up his religion, and promise to be a Papist. As soon as he had been so weak as to do this, his enemies ordered him to be burned at Oxford. When he was taken to be tied to the stake, he stretched out his right hand that it might burn first, because it had written through fear what he did not truly believe. He took off all his clothes but his shirt, as all those martyrs had to do, and with a cheerful countenance he began to praise God aloud, and to pray for pardon for the faults he might have committed during a long life. His patience in bearing the torment of burning, and his courage in dying, made all people love him as much as it made them hate the queen and Bonner.

Nothing did well in this queen's reign. She went to war with France to please her husband the king of Spain, and in that war the French took Calais from the English, who had kept it ever since Edward the Third's reign.*

Queen Mary died the same year in which she lost Calais, after being queen for only five years.

* Little Arthur should look back, and read the story of the taking of Calais, and of the good Eustace de St. Pierre.

CHAPTER XLIV

ELIZABETH—1558 TO 1603

Queen Elizabeth's reign was so very long, and there are so many things in it to tell you about, that I am sure we must have three chapters about her, and you will find both good and bad in them ; but after all you will think that her being queen was a very good thing for England.

When Queen Mary died, Elizabeth was at Hatfield, where she stayed a little while, till some of the great and wise men belonging to the country went to her to advise her what she had best do for the good of England, and how she should begin. At the end of a week she went to London.

She was twenty-five years old, and very pleasant looking. She was a good scholar in Latin, Greek, Italian, and some other languages ; but she loved English above all.

The first thing Elizabeth and her wise counsellors did was to set free all the poor Protestants whom Queen Mary and Bishop Bonner had put in prison, and intended to burn. Then she allowed the Bible and prayers to be read in English.

When Elizabeth rode through London to be crowned in Westminster Abbey, the citizens made all sorts of fine shows to do honour to a queen who had already been so good to the poor Protestants, and who wished to be good to all in England. They hung beautiful silks and satins out at the windows like flags ; they built fine wooden arches across the streets, which they dressed up with branches of trees and flowers ; and just as the queen was riding under one of them, a boy beautifully dressed was let down by cords from the top, who gave the queen a beautiful Bible, and then he was drawn up again. Elizabeth took the Bible and kissed it, and pressed it to her bosom, and said it was a present she liked best of all the fine things the people had given her that day.

Afterwards she appointed Protestant bishops, and made a very good and earnest man, named Matthew Parker, Archbishop of Canterbury.

Queen Elizabeth did not find it easy to undo all the mischief that Queen Mary had done ; but at last, with the help of her counsellors, England was at peace, and the people were settled, some on their lands, where they were beginning to sow more corn and make more gardens than they had done before, and some in different trades ; for the English learned to make a great many things at this time from strangers that came to live here.

I will tell you why they came. That cruel Philip the Second, King of Spain, who had been married to Queen Mary, was King over Flanders and Holland, as well as Spain. A great many of the people in those countries were Protestants ; but Philip wanted to make them Papists by force, and would have burnt them as Queen Mary did the Protestants in England. But they got away from him, and hearing that Queen Elizabeth was a friend to the Protestants they came here. And as some of them were spinners and weavers, and others dyers, and so on, they began to work at their trades, and taught them to the English. Since that time we have always been able to make woollen and linen cloth ourselves.

So you see that King Philip, by being cruel, drove away useful people from his country, and Queen Elizabeth, by being kind and just, got those useful people to do good to our own dear England.

I must tell you a sad story of the worst thing that happened in Queen Elizabeth's time, in this chapter, because it has a great deal to do with the Protestants and Papists.

In the chapter about Edward the Sixth you read that there was a beautiful young Queen of Scotland, and that the English wished King Edward to marry her ; but that she went to France, and married the young French king instead.

She was so very young when she first went, that her husband's mother kept her to teach along with her own little girls till she was old enough to be married ; and I am sorry to say that she taught her to be worldly and deceitful.

Her name was Mary, and she was the most beautiful young queen in the world ; and the old French queen, whose name was Catherine, taught her to love dress, and shows, and dancing, more than anything, although she was so clever that she might have learned all the good things that the beautiful Lady Jane Grey had learned.

The young King of France died very soon, and then Mary, who is always called Queen of Scots, went home to Scotland. If she had been wise, she might have done as much good as her cousin Queen Elizabeth did in England.

But she had been too long living in gaiety and amusement in France, to know what was best for her people ; and instead of listening to good counsellors, as Elizabeth did, she would take advice from nobody but Frenchmen, or others who would dance and sing instead of minding serious things.

When she went away from Scotland all the people were Papists ; but long before she got back, not only the people, but most of the great lords, were Protestants ; and Mary was very much vexed, and tried to make them all turn Papists again.

At last, there was a civil war in Scotland, between the Papists and Protestants, which did much mischief : at the end of it, the Protestants promised Mary to let her be a Papist, and have Papist clergymen for herself and the lords and ladies belonging to her house ; and she promised that her children should be brought up as Protestants, and that the people should be allowed to worship God in the way they liked best.

Just before this war Mary had married her cousin, Henry Stuart, called Lord Darnley, who was very weak and wilful ; but she liked him very much indeed for a little time, and they had a son called James. But soon afterwards Mary was much offended with Darnley, and showed great favour to Lord Bothwell. Not long afterwards Lord Bothwell murdered Darnley at the very time when Mary was giving a ball in her palace and was dancing merrily ; and most people then thought that Mary had planned the wicked deed with Bothwell that she might be able to marry him.

And it turned out just as everybody expected ; so you cannot wonder that most of those who were good were very angry indeed when they found that she chose to marry that wicked man three months after he had killed her poor husband.

Then there was another civil war, and Mary was put into prison in Loch Leven Castle, which stands on a little island in the middle of a lake. However, by the help of one of her friends she got out, and once more got her Papist advisers round her, who tried to make her queen again.

But the Scots would not allow it, and they made her little infant James their king, and made the lords Murray and

Morton, and some others, guardians for the little king and the kingdom.

It would have been well for Queen Mary if she would have lived in Scotland quietly, and taken care of her little son herself. But her bad husband, Bothwell, had run away to save his own life, and Mary Queen of Scots chose to come to England, in hopes that Queen Elizabeth, her cousin, would help her to get the kingdom of Scotland again.

I cannot tell you all the things that happened to Mary Queen of Scots in England. But I must say that I wish she had never come. She first of all seemed to want to make friends with Elizabeth, but all the time she was sending letters to the kings of France and Spain, to ask them to help her to get not only Scotland, but England for herself, and she promised one of the great English lords she would marry him, and make him king, if he would help her too.

She also sent to get the Pope's help, and promised that all the people in England and Scotland too should be Papists, and obey the Pope again, and send him a great deal of money every year, if she could only kill or drive away Queen Elizabeth.

Now, Elizabeth's faithful friends and counsellors found out all these letters to the Pope and the kings of France and Spain, and they were so afraid lest any harm should happen to their good, useful Queen Elizabeth, that they kept Mary Queen of Scots in prison, sometimes in one great castle, sometimes in another.

They allowed her to walk, and ride, and to have her ladies and other friends with her, and many people visited her at first. But when it was known that she really wished to make the English all Papists again, she was not allowed to see so many people.

At last—I could almost cry when I tell you of it—the beautiful, and clever, and very unhappy Queen of Scots was ordered to be beheaded ! She was in prison at Fotheringay Castle when Queen Elizabeth's cruel order to cut off her head was sent to her. The next day her steward and her ladies led her into the great hall of the castle, which was hung all round with black cloth. In the middle of the hall there was a place raised above the floor, also covered with black. There her maids took off her veil, and she knelt down and laid her beautiful head on the block. It was cut off, and her servants took it and her body to bury.

Mary had done many wicked things : she had tried to do much mischief in England. But as she was not born in England, but was the queen of another country, neither Elizabeth nor her counsellors had any right either to keep her in prison, or to put her to death. They ought to have sent her, at the very first, safely to some other country, if they were really afraid she would do mischief in England.

This is a very bad thing : and I cannot make any excuse for Elizabeth. I will only say that her old counsellors were so afraid lest Mary should prevail on the kings of France and Spain to help her to kill Elizabeth, and make the English all Papists again, that they wished Elizabeth to have ordered Mary's head to be taken off long before she really did so.

CHAPTER XLV

ELIZABETH—(*continued*)

It is quite pleasant, my little friend, to have to write a chapter for you, where I can tell you of all things going well for England, that dear country where God allows us to live, which He has given us to love, and to do all we can for.

When first Elizabeth became queen, her counsellors and the parliament, and the people, all asked her to marry, and promised to receive kindly anybody she should choose. And the King of Spain asked her to marry him, but she told him he would not marry him, because he had been her sister's husband ; and she did not believe the Pope had power to allow her to marry one who had been her sister's husband. Then the old Queen of France, Catherine of Medicis, who had taught poor Mary Queen of Scots to be so foolish and cruel, wanted Queen Elizabeth to marry one of her sons. But Elizabeth did not like them any better than she did Philip, yet more than once she pretended she was going to marry one of them, for she wanted to be friends with France, and so make England strong and able to fight successfully against Spain. Then some of the great English lords wanted to marry her. But she knew that if she married one of them the others would be jealous, and, may be, would make a civil war in England ; so she thanked the counsellors, and the Parliament, and the people, for their kindness, but said she would rather live single, as she had quite enough to do to govern the kingdom well, without being troubled with marrying. And she kept her word, and never married, and is always called the Maiden Queen.

I told you long ago, that the first great sea-fight in which the English beat the French was in the reign of Edward the Third. Since that time the English ships had been very much improved ; instead of only one mast, the largest had three, and instead of stones for the sailors to throw at their enemies, there were large and small guns to fight with. Then the sailors were as much improved as the ships. Instead of only sailing along by the land, and only going to sea in good weather, they made long voyages.

You know, in the reign of Queen Elizabeth's grandfather, I told you that some bold sailors had sailed so far as America. Now Queen Elizabeth, who knew very well that the kings of France and Spain wanted to make war upon England, and drive her away, and oppress the Protestants, thought, like wise King Alfred, that the best way to defend England was to have plenty of ships and good seamen, and brave admirals and captains to command them ; and so meet her enemies on the sea, and keep them from ever landing in England.

I must tell you something about one or two of Queen Elizabeth's great admirals.

Sir Francis Drake, the first man who ever sailed his ship round the whole world, was born in Devonshire, and went to sea at first with some other brave gentlemen to carry on a war against some towns which the Spaniards had built in South America. This was very wrong, because private persons have no business to make war, and take towns, and make prisoners of the townspeople. Such things should only be done when there is a lawful war between two countries. Then, indeed, every man must do his duty, and fight as well as he can for his own country and king. If private gentlemen were to go and take towns belonging to other countries, now, they would be called pirates, and they would be hanged.

However, as Sir Francis Drake grew older, he left off making private war, became one of the queen's best admirals, and you will read more about him near the end of this chapter.

When he made his grand voyage round the world, he sailed always from the East to the West. He first went round Cape Horn, at the very South end of South America, where he saw great islands of ice as high as a large hill, and penguins and albatrosses swimming about them. Then he sailed to the Spice Islands, where he saw cloves and nutmegs grow, and birds of Paradise flying about in the air, and peacocks in the fields, and monkeys skipping from tree to tree in the woods. Then he passed by the Cape of Good Hope, which is in the South part of Africa, where all the beautiful geraniums and heaths come from.

Queen Elizabeth spoke to him kindly when he set out, and when he came back, after being three years at sea, she went and dined with him on board his own ship, and saw all the beautiful and curious things he had brought home with him.

Another great Admiral was Sir Martin Frobisher, who had been to the farthest parts of North America, and first saw all the land about Hudson's Bay, and those countries to the south of that bay, where the English not long afterwards built towns, and settled a great many free states, that you will read a great deal about some day.

In many things, the next admiral I will tell you about was a greater man than any of the rest. His name was Sir Walter Raleigh ; he was both a sailor and a soldier : sometimes he commanded a ship, and sometimes he fought along with the army on shore.

7*

The first time the queen took notice of him was one day that she was walking in London, and came to a splashy place just as Sir Walter was going by. As she was thinking how she could best step through the mud, Sir Walter took off a nice new cloak that he had on, and spread it on the dirt, so that the queen might walk over without wetting her shoes. She was very much pleased, and desired him to go to see her at her palace ; and as she found that he was very clever and very brave, she made him one of her chief admirals.

Queen Elizabeth used to behave to her brave admirals and generals, and her wise counsellors, and even to her great merchants, like a friend. She visited them in their houses, and talked to them cheerfully of her affairs. She took notice of even the poorest people, and she used to walk and ride about, so that all her subjects knew her and loved her. And now I am going to tell you a part of her history, which will show you how happy it was for her and for England that the people did love their good queen.

The King of Spain had never loved Elizabeth ; and he hated England, because the people were Protestants : and I am sure you remember how cruel he was, and bitter in his religion.

He made war against England, and thought that if he could land a great army on the coast, he might conquer all the country and drive away Elizabeth, and make the English all Papists again. He hoped this would be easy, because he was the richest king in the world, and had more ships and sailors and soldiers than any other. And he began to build more ships and to collect more sailors and soldiers ; and he made so sure he should conquer England, that I have heard he even had chains put on board the ships, to chain the English admirals when his people should take them.

This fleet, that King Philip made ready to conquer England, was the largest that any king had ever sent to sea, and he called it the " Invincible Armada," * because, he said, nobody could conquer it.

But Queen Elizabeth heard in time that Philip was making ready this great navy, to bring as great an army to attack England. She immediately told the Parliament and people of her danger. She rode out herself to see her soldiers and her ships, and she said she trusted herself entirely to her good people. The people soon showed her they might be trusted : they came willingly to be sailors and soldiers ; and the great lords gave money to pay the soldiers ; and many gentlemen built ships, and bought guns, and gave them to the queen. And she had soon a good fleet. It was not so large as King Philip's indeed, and the ships were quite small compared with his ; but the sailors belonging to it remembered that they were to fight for their own dear England, and for a queen whom they loved.

The chief admiral was Lord Howard of Effingham ; and to show how true Englishmen can be, and should be, when their country is in danger, although he was a Roman Catholic he was glad to fight for England against Spain. Under him were Lord Seymour, Sir Francis Drake, Sir John Hawkins, Sir Martin Frobisher, Sir Walter Raleigh, and several other lords and gentlemen.

The queen got ready herself to march to whatever place the Spaniards might land at. She had a good army a little way from London, at Tilbury Fort, and she went there on horseback, and spoke to the soldiers, to give them courage.

Oh, how anxious everybody in England was, when the news came that the great Armada was at sea, and sailing very

* Armada is the Spanish word for Navy.

The Spanish Armada.

near them ! but it pleased God to save England. Soon after the Spanish fleet set sail a great storm arose, and many of the ships were so damaged that they could not come to England at all.

Queen Elizabeth reviewing her army at Tilbury.

When the others did come, Queen Elizabeth's fleet sailed out and followed them for a week up the English Channel, fighting and beating them all the way. At last, in the Straits of Dover, the English admirals sent fire ships into the middle of the Armada, and the Spaniards sailed away in a fright ; and not one ship got to England to land Spanish soldiers. Twelve of them were taken or destroyed; and another storm, greater than the first, sank a great many and wrecked others, so that of all Philip's great fleet and army, only one-third could get back to Spain; and they were so tired and so hurt that he never could get them together again to attack England, although in his hatred of our country he still hoped to do so.

Philip must have been very sorry that he began to make war against England, for the war lasted as long as he lived, and every year the English admirals used to take a good many of his ships; and one year Lord Essex, who was a great favourite of Queen Elizabeth's, landed in Spain, and took Cadiz, one of Philip's best towns, and burnt a great many ships that were in its harbour.

CHAPTER XLVI

ELIZABETH—(*continued*)

It is a long time since I mentioned Ireland to you. You know that in the reign of King Henry the Second the English took a great part of it, and drove the old Irish away to the west side of the island.

Now the English, who settled in Ireland at that time, soon grew more like Irish than Englishmen, and they were as ready to quarrel with any new English that went to settle there as the old Irish had been to quarrel with them ; so poor Ireland had never been quiet. The different lords of the new Irish, and the kings of the old were always fighting, and then they sent to England sometimes to ask for help, and often to complain of one another. Then the kings of England used to send soldiers, with private captains, who very often fought whoever they met, instead of helping one side or the other ; and these soldiers generally treated the unhappy Irish as ill as the Danes used to treat the English.

In Queen Elizabeth's time the miserable people in Ireland were never a day without some sad quarrel or fight in which many people were killed ; and though Ireland is a good country for corn and cattle, and all things useful, yet there was nothing to be had there but oatmeal ; the people lived like wild savages, and even a good many of the English that had settled there wore the coarse Irish dress, used bows and arrows, and let their hair grow filthy and matted, more like the wild old Britons you read of in the first chapter, than like Christian gentlemen.

Ireland was strangely divided then ; there was the part where the old Irish lived in huts among bogs and mountains ; then the part with a few old castles that the first English settlers had built ; and then that part where fresh captains, who had come from time to time, had fixed themselves in forts and towns ; and all these parts were constantly at war.

Elizabeth, when she found how very ill Ireland was governed, wished to make it a little more like England, and to try to bring the people to live in peace. She sent a wise Governor there, called Sir Henry Sydney, and then another called Arthur Lord Grey de Wilton ; but all that these good men could do was to keep the new English a little in order, and to try to do justice to the other people. By the queen's orders they set up schools, and a college in Dublin, in hopes that the young Irishmen would learn to become more like the men of other countries.

But the bad way of governing Ireland had gone on too long to allow it to be changed all at once ; and Elizabeth found she must send an army there to keep the different English and Irish chiefs in order, if she wished to have peace in the country.

Now these chiefs were all Roman Catholics, for I believe there were no Protestants in Ireland but the very newest of the English ; and when the King of Spain made war against Queen Elizabeth, he sent some Spanish soldiers to Ireland to help the Irish chiefs to make war upon the English.

The story of these wars is long and very sad, and belongs rightly to the history of Ireland ; but I must tell you what happened to one or two of the chief men of Ireland at this time.

The Earl of Desmond was one who joined the King of Spain's people, and when Lord Grey drove the Spaniards out of Ireland, Desmond tried to hide himself among the woods and bogs in the wildest part of the country. But the English soldiers hunted him from place to place, so that he had no rest. One night he and his wife had just gone to bed in a house close by the side of a river; the English soldiers came, and the old Lord and Lady Desmond had just time to get up and run into the water, in which they stood up to their necks, till the English were gone. At last some soldiers, who were seeking for them, saw a very old man sitting by himself in a poor hut: they found out it was the Earl of Desmond, and they cut off his head directly, and sent it to Queen Elizabeth.

But the most famous Irishman at this time was Hugh O'Neill, Earl of Tyrone. His uncle, Shane O'Neill, tried to make himself King of Ulster, and hated the English so that he killed some of his own family because they wanted to teach the Irish to eat bread like the English, instead of oat cakes.

This Hugh, Earl of Tyrone, had a large army of Irish, and fought all the queen's officers for many years, though she sent many of the best and bravest there. Sir Henry Bagenal was one, and her greatest favourite, the Earl of Essex, was another. Two or three times, when Tyrone was near being conquered, he pretended to submit, and promised that if the queen would forgive him, he would keep his Irish friends quiet. He broke his word, however, and kept a civil war up in Ireland till very near the queen's death, when, after being almost starved for want of food in the bogs near his own home, he made peace in earnest, and Ireland was quiet for a few years.

We are now come to the end of Queen Elizabeth's long and famous reign. She died when she had been queen forty-five years, and was very unhappy at her death. Her favourite Lord Essex behaved so ill after he came from Ireland, that the queen's counsellors ordered him to be put to death. Now, the queen had once given him a ring, when he was her greatest favourite, and told him, that if he would send it to her whenever he was in danger, she would save his life and forgive any of his faults. She thought he would send this ring to her, when he knew he was condemned to have his head cut off : and so he did ; but a cruel woman to whom he trusted it, to give the queen, never did so till long after Essex was dead ; and then Elizabeth, who was old and ill herself, was so vexed, that she hardly ever spoke to anybody again, and died in a few days afterwards at Richmond.

It would make our little history too long, if I tried to tell you of all the wise and good things done by Elizabeth, or if I told you the names of half the famous men who lived in her time.

Besides Essex, there was her other favourite, Leicester, a clever bad man.

Her god-son, Harrington, belonged to the learned men and poets of her time ; but neither he nor any of the rest, though there were many, were to be compared to Shakespeare, whose plays everybody reads and loves, nor even to Spenser or to Marlowe, who lived and died in Elizabeth's reign.

Then there were her wise counsellors Sir Nicholas Bacon, Lord Burleigh, and Walsingham, and all the generals and admirals I have told you about. I must just mention one more, because you will wish to be like him when you grow up. He was Sir Philip Sidney, the best and wisest, and most learned, and bravest. He was killed in battle. When he was lying on the ground, very hot and thirsty, and bleeding to death, a friend was bringing him a cup of water ; but he happened to look round, and saw a poor dying soldier who had no friends near him, looking eagerly towards the cup. Sir Philip did not touch it, but sent it to be given to that soldier, who blessed him as he was dying. And that act of self-denial and mercy makes all who hear the name of Philip Sidney bless him even now.

CHAPTER XLVII

JAMES I.—1603 TO 1625

James Stuart, the first King James of England, but the sixth of Scotland, was one of the most foolish and mischievous kings we ever had in England. He was the son of the unhappy Mary Queen of Scots, and after she was put in prison the first time, the Scottish lords made James king, though he was quite an infant. The lords gave him the best masters they could find to teach him, and he learned what was in books very well, but nobody could ever teach him how to behave well or wisely.

When Queen Elizabeth died, James, king of Scotland, became king of England, because he was Elizabeth's cousin, and from that time England and Scotland have been under one king, and are called the United Kingdom of Great Britain.

As soon as James heard the queen was dead, he set out from Scotland to come to London ; for as Scotland was then a very poor country, he and a great number of Scotsmen who came with him thought they had nothing to do but to come to England, and get all the money they could by all sorts of ways. Then he made so many lords and knights that people began to laugh at him and his new nobles. But, worst of all, he fancied that parliaments had no business to prevent kings from doing whatever they pleased, and taking money from their subjects whenever they liked.

You may think how vexed the English were when they found that they had a king so unfit for them, after their wise Queen Elizabeth.

The queen of James was Anne, the daughter of the king of Denmark. She was extravagant, and loved feasts and balls, and acted plays herself, and filled the court with rioting, instead of the lady-like music and dancing, and poetry and needlework, that Queen Elizabeth and her ladies loved.

Instead of riding about among the people, and depending on their love and good-will, James was always hiding himself; the only thing he seemed to love was hunting, and for the sake of that he neglected his people and his business.

The favourites he had were far from being useful, or wise, or brave. He chose them for their good looks and fine appearance, without inquiring anything about their behaviour.

He dealt severely with the Roman Catholics, whom he put in prison, and from whom he took a great deal of money. Then he disliked those Protestants who did not wish to have bishops as well as parish clergymen, and who are mostly called Presbyterians; but some were then named Puritans, and he would not let them alter the Prayer-book.

The Roman Catholics being tired of the ill usage they got from King James, some of them thought that, if they could kill him, they might take one of his young children to bring up themselves, and have a Roman Catholic king or queen, and get all England and Scotland for themselves. They thought besides, that they had better kill all the lords and all the gentlemen of the House of Commons too, and so get rid of the whole Protestant parliament.

From thinking wickedly they went on to do wickedly. They found there were some cellars under the houses of parliament, and they filled these cellars with gunpowder ; and as they expected the parliament would meet in the house all together, with the king, on the fifth day of November, they hired a man called Guy Fawkes to set fire to the gunpowder, and so to blow it up, and kill everybody there at once.

Now, it happened that one of the lords, whose name was Mounteagle, had a friend among the Roman Catholics, and that friend wrote him a letter, without signing his name, to beg him not to go to the parliament that day, for that a sudden blow would be struck which would destroy them all. Lord Mounteagle took this letter to the king's council. Some of the councillors laughed at it, and said it was only sent to frighten Lord Mounteagle. But the king took it, and after thinking a little, he said, the sudden blow must mean something to be done with gunpowder, and he set people to watch who went in and out of the vaults under the parliament-house ; till at last, on the very night before those conspirators hoped to kill the king and all those belonging to parliament, they caught Guy Fawkes with his dark lantern, waiting till the time should come for him to set fire to the gunpowder.

The king was very proud of having found out what the letter meant, and used to boast of it as long as he lived ; but the truth is that the king's clever minister, Sir Robert Cecil, had found out all about the plot, and managed to let James have all the credit.

So far I have only told you of the foolish behaviour of King James. I must now write about his mischievous actions.

His eldest son, Prince Henry, died very young ; he was a sensible lad, and the people were sorry when he died, expecially as his brother Charles was a sickly little boy.

Now, little Charles was a clever child, and had very good

dispositions ; and if he had been properly brought up, he might have been a good king, and a happy man. Instead of that, you will read that he was a bad king, and I daresay you will cry when you find how very unhappy he was at last.

James taught him that no power on earth had any right to find fault with the king, that the king's power was given to him by God, and that it was a great sin to say that anything the king did was wrong. Thus he taught him to think that the people were made for nothing but to obey kings, and to labour and get money for kings to spend as they pleased, and that even the nobles were nothing but servants for kings ; in short, he filled his poor little son's mind with wrong thoughts, and never taught him that it was a king's duty to do all the good he could for his people, and to set an example of what is right.

Yet Charles had many good qualities, as you will read by and by. He was a good scholar, and loved books and clever men, and music, and pictures ; and if he had only been taught his duty as a king properly, he would have done a great deal of good to England.

I have told you that James used to make favourites of people, without caring much about their goodness. One of his greatest favourites was George Villiers, Duke of Buckingham, and he gave his son Charles to the duke to take care of, just when he was grown up. The silly king used to call Buckingham, Steenie, and the prince, Baby Charles, although he was almost as big and as old as a man.

When the prince was old enough to have a wife, his father wished him to marry the Infanta of Spain. (In Spain the princes are called Infants, and the princesses Infantas.) Now the Duke of Buckingham wanted very much to go abroad, and show himself to all the princes and nobles in France and

Spain, for he was very vain of his beauty and his fine clothes ; so he put it into the prince's head to tell his father he would not marry unless he would let him go to Spain with the Duke of Buckingham, and see the Infanta before he married her.

King James I. with Steenie and Baby Charles.

The poor foolish king began crying like a child, and begged his dear Steenie and Baby Charles not to go and leave him ; but they laughed at him, and went and borrowed all his fine diamonds and pearls, to wear in their hats and round their necks, and took all the money they could get, and set off to go to Spain. They called themselves John Smith and Thomas Smith, and first they went to France.

Prince Charles found the ladies in the French court very pleasant and entertaining. It is true that several of them were not very good, but then they amused Charles, and he was particularly pleased with the Princess Henrietta Maria, who was pretty and merry, and appeared to like Charles very much.

They quickly pursued their journey through France to go to Spain, and when Charles and Buckingham first got there everything seemed very pleasant. The Infanta was handsome, but very different from Henrietta Maria, for she was very grave and steady, and seemed as if she would be a fit wife for the prince, who was naturally grave and steady too.

But the Duke of Buckingham quarrelled with some of the great men of the court, and was so much affronted at not being treated rather like a king than only a plain English nobleman, that he made the prince believe that the King of Spain meant to offend him, and did not really intend his daughter to marry him ; and, in short, he contrived to make Charles so angry, that he left Spain in a rage, and afterwards married that very French princess, Henrietta Maria, whom he had seen at Paris.

The bad education King James gave his son Charles, though it was the most mischievous of all his bad acts, was not the only one.

The King of Spain had taken a dislike to Sir Walter Raleigh, who had been so great a favourite of Queen Elizabeth, because Raleigh had beaten his sailors at sea, and his soldiers ashore. But Sir Walter's men happened to kill some Spaniards when they were looking for a gold mine in

South America; so the King of Spain demanded that James should put Raleigh to death, and James shamefully yielded to Spain, and ordered that great and wise man's head to be cut off.

As to Scotland, King James's own country, he behaved as ill in all things belonging to it as he did in England. But the thing that turned out worst for the country and his poor son Charles was his insisting on the Scottish people kneeling at the communion, keeping certain holy days, and having bishops, although the Scotch religion is presbyterian. This vexed the Scottish people very much indeed. And the Irish were not better pleased, because the Roman Catholics were ill-treated by James, and most of the Irish were Roman Catholics.

When James died, all the three kingdoms of England, Scotland, and Ireland were discontented. Poor Ireland was even worse off than ever. Scotland had been neglected, and the people affronted about their religion; and, in England, James had taken money unlawfully, and behaved so ill both to parliament and people, that everybody disliked him as a king, and he was so silly in his private behaviour, that everybody laughed at him as a gentleman.

In short, I can praise him for nothing but a little book-learning; but as he made no good use of it, he might almost as well have been without it. He reigned twenty-two years in England, during which there was no great war. But James had begun one against the Emperor of Germany and the King of Spain, just before his death.

I must tell you of one very great man who lived in his reign, Lord Bacon. He was one of the wisest men that ever lived, though not without his faults, but when you grow up you will read his books if you wish to be truly wise.

CHAPTER XLVIII

CHARLES I.—1625 TO 1649

When Charles the First came to be king, all the people were in hopes that he would be a better king than his father, as they believed he was a better man, and so he really was.

He was young and pleasant-looking; he was fond of learning, and seemed inclined to show kindness to all clever men, whether they were poets or good writers in any way, or musicians, or painters, or architects.

Besides, the people hoped that he would manage his money better than James, and not waste it in clothes, and jewels, and drinking, and hunting, and giving it to favourites.

But, unhappily, Charles still allowed the Duke of Buckingham to advise him in everything; indeed, he was a greater favourite than before James's death, for he had managed to get the French princess Henrietta Maria for a wife for Charles, who was so fond of her, that he thought he never could thank Buckingham enough for bringing her to England.

But the parliament, particularly the Commons, did not like the marriage so much. The new queen was a Roman Catholic, and she brought a number of Roman Catholic ladies and priests to be her servants, and she soon showed that she was greedy and extravagant.

Charles, who, as I told you, had been very badly taught by his father, desired the parliament to give him money in a very haughty manner. The parliament said the people should pay some taxes, but that they could not afford a great deal at that time, for James had been so extravagant that they had not much left to give. Charles, by the advice of Buckingham, sent away the parliament, and tried to get money without its leave, and sent officers about the country to beg for money in the king's name. Most people were afraid to refuse, and so Charles and Buckingham got a good deal, to do as they pleased with.

Buckingham persuaded King Charles to make war against France, because one of the great men in France had affronted him. King James had begun a war with Spain.

The people were now more and more angry, for though they might like to fight for the glory and safety of England, or for the good of the king, they could not bear to think of fighting for a proud, cruel, and selfish man like Buckingham.

I do not know what might have happened at that very time, perhaps a civil war, if a desperate man named Felton had not killed the Duke of Buckingham at Portsmouth, when he was on the way to France to renew the war.

The people were again in hopes that the king would do what was right, and consult the parliament before he attempted to make war, or take money from his subjects, or put any man in prison, now that his bad adviser, Buckingham, was dead. But they were much mistaken. Charles found new advisers, and governed for eleven years without a parliament. The king wanted money, and tried to compel all who had land to pay a tax called Ship Money ; but some gentlemen, one of whom was Mr. John Hampden, refused to pay it, and said it was unlawful for the king to take money without the consent of parliament. But the judges declared that the king could take Ship Money, and that the people must pay it. Two of them, however, felt compelled to say that Charles had broken the laws, and the promises made by the English kings in agreement with the Great Charter.

This made the people very angry. They said the worst times were come again, when the kings fancied they might rob their subjects, and put them in prison when they pleased.

Charles was a very affectionate man, and he could not help loving and trusting others instead of making use of his own sense and trusting his people, as Queen Elizabeth had done. So he allowed the queen to advise him in most things, and Laud, Bishop of London, in others; particularly in matters of religion. So he began to oppress the Puritans in England. In poor Ireland, a harsh man, the Earl of Strafford, a great friend and favourite of King Charles, governed in such a cruel manner that everybody complained.

He sent English clergymen to preach in those parts of Ireland where the poor people could only understand Irish, and punished the people for not listening: and when some of the bishops (particularly good Bishop Bedel) begged him to have mercy upon the Irish, he threatened to punish them most severely for speaking in their favour.

All this time the king and queen and their friends were going on taking money by unlawful means from the people, till he was obliged to call a parliament. Then the gentlemen of the Commons insisted on Lord Strafford and Archbishop Laud being punished. Indeed, they would not be satisfied until Charles consented that Strafford's head should be cut off.

Now, though Strafford well deserved some punishment, he had done nothing which by law deserved death; and therefore Charles ought to have refused his consent. The king had often quarrelled with the parliament, and acted contrary to its advice when he was in the wrong; but now that it would have been right to resist he gave way, and

Strafford going to Execution.

Strafford, who loved Charles, and whose very faults were owing to the king's own wishes and commands, was beheaded by his order.

This was a sad thing for Charles. His friends found that he could not defend them, and many went away from England. The king still wanted to take money, and govern in all things, without the parliament ; he even went so far as to send some of the Commons to prison. And the parliament became so angry at last that a dreadful civil war began.

The king put himself at the head of one army, and his nephew, Prince Rupert, a brave but rash man, came from Germany to assist him. The queen went to France and Holland, to try to get foreign soldiers to fight in the king's army against the parliament. The king's people were called Cavaliers.

The parliament soon gathered another army together to fight the king, and made Lord Essex general ; and the navy also joined the parliament : and the parliament people, because of the way their hair was cropped whereas the Cavaliers wore their hair long, were called Roundheads.

Now we will end this chapter. And I beg you will think of what I said about James the First, that he was a mischievous king. If he had not begun to behave ill to the people and parliament, and taught his son Charles that there was no occasion for kings to keep the laws, these quarrels with the parliament need not have happened, and there would not have been a Civil War.

CHAPTER XLIX

CHARLES I.—(continued)

A book twice as big as our little History would not hold all the story of the Civil Wars. England, Scotland, and Ireland were all engaged in them ; and many dreadful battles were fought, where Englishmen killed one another, and a great deal of blood was shed.

The first great battle was fought at Edgehill, where many of the king's officers were killed : then, at a less fight at Chalgrove, the parliament lost that great and good man, Mr. Hampden. The battles of Newbury, of Marston Moor, and of Naseby, are all sadly famous for the number of brave and good Englishmen that were killed.

During this civil war, the parliament sent often to the king, in hopes of persuading him to make peace : and I believe that the parliament, and the king, and the real English lords and gentlemen on both sides, truly desired to have peace, and several times the king had promised the parliament to do what they lawfully might ask of him.

But, unhappily, the queen had come back to England, and the king trusted her and took her advice, when he had much better have followed his own good thoughts. Now, the queen and Prince Rupert, the king's nephew, and some of the lords, were of James the First's way of thinking, and would not allow that subjects had any right even to their own lives, or lands, or money, if the king chose to take them and so they persuaded the king to break his word so often with the people and parliament, that at last they could not trust him any longer.

When the king found that the parliament would not trust him again, he determined to go to the Scottish army that had come to England to help the parliament, and he hoped that the Scots would take his part and defend him. But he had offended the Scots by meddling more than they liked with their religion, and some other things, and the leaders of their army agreed to give him up to the English parliament. You will hardly believe, however, that those mean Scots actually sold the king to the English parliament : but they did so. The unhappy king was sent back to England, and was now obliged to agree to what the parliament wished, and there seemed to be an end of the Civil War.

It was not long, however, before it began again, and this second time it ended in Cromwell and the other generals of the army becoming the most powerful men in England. These men now drove away almost all the lords and gentlemen from parliament, so there was nobody but the soldiers who had any power.

The wisest of the generals, Lord Essex, was dead. The next, General Fairfax, was a good man, but neither so clever nor so prudent as some of the others, particularly one whose name was Oliver Cromwell.

This Cromwell was a Puritan, or Roundhead. He was brave and very sagacious, and strictly religious, according to his own notions, though his enemies thought him a hypocrite.

He may have thought that, though the army had got King Charles in its power, the people would never allow him to be put in prison for his lifetime, and that, if he were sent away to another country, he might come back sometime and make war again. So he said that the king had behaved so ill that

8

he ought to be tried before judges. And he and the other generals named a great many judges to examine into all the king's actions and words.

In the mean time King Charles had been moved from one prison to another, till at last he was brought to London to be tried.

I cannot explain to you, my dear, all the hard and cruel things that were done to this poor king, whose greatest faults were owing to the bad education given him by his father, and the bad advice he got from his wife, and those men whom he thought were his best friends.

When his misfortunes came, his wife escaped to France with a few of her own favourites, and her eldest son, Charles, Prince of Wales, also escaped. Soon after his second son, James, Duke of York, also escaped, to his mother ; but the king's daughter, Princess Elizabeth, and the little Henry, Duke of Gloucester, remained in England.

When King Charles was brought to London, only two of his own friends could see him every day ; one of these was Dr. Juxon, Bishop of London, and the other was Mr. Herbert, his valet, who had been with him ever since the army had made him prisoner.

Shortly after the king was brought to London the judges appointed by the army condemned him to death, and three days afterwards his head was cut off.

But those three days were the best and greatest of Charles's life. In those he showed that, if he had been mistaken as a king, he was a good man and a right high-minded gentleman. One of these days you will read and know more about him. I will only tell you now about his taking leave of his children ; and I will copy the very words of his valet, Mr. Herbert, who wrote down all that happened to his dear king and master, during the last days of his life.

The day after the king was condemned to die, " Princess
Elizabeth and the Duke of Gloucester, her brother, came to
take their sad farewell of the king their father, and to ask his
blessing. This was the twenty-ninth of January. The Princess, being the elder, was the most sensible of her royal
father's condition, as appeared by her sorrowful look and
excessive weeping ; and her little brother seeing his sister

Parting of King Charles and his children.

weep, he took the like impression, though, by reason of
his tender age, he could not have the like apprehensions.
The king raised them both from off their knees ; he kissed
them, gave them his blessing, and setting them on his knees,
admonished them concerning their duty and loyal observance
to the queen their mother, the prince that was his successor,
love to the Duke of York and his other relations. The king

then gave them all his jewels, save the George he wore, which was cut out in an onyx with great curiosity, and set about with twenty-one fair diamonds, and the reverse set with the like number ; and again kissing his children, had such pretty

King Charles I. on the Scaffold.

and pertinent answers from them both, as drew tears of joy and love from his eyes ; and then, praying God Almighty to bless them, he turned about, expressing a tender and fatherly affection. Most sorrowful was this parting, the young princess shedding tears and crying lamentably, so as moved others to pity that formerly were hard-hearted ; and at opening the chamber-door, the king returned hastily from the window and kissed them and blessed them." So this poor little prince and princess never saw their father again.

The next morning very early, the king called Mr. Herbert to help him to dress, and said it was like a second marriage-day, and he wished to be well dressed, for before night he hoped to be in heaven.

While he was dressing, he said, " Death is not terrible to me ! I bless God that I am prepared." Good Bishop Juxon then came and prayed with Charles, till Colonel Hacker, who had the care of the king, came to call them.

Then the king walked to Whitehall, and as he went one soldier prayed " God bless " him. And so he passed to the banqueting house, in front of which a scaffold was built. King Charles was brought out upon it ; and after speaking a short time to his friends, and to good Bishop Juxon, he knelt down and laid his head upon the block, and a man in a mask cut off his head with one stroke.

The bishop and Mr. Herbert then took their master's body and head, and laid them in a coffin, and buried them in St. George's Chapel at Windsor, where several kings had been buried before.

CHAPTER L

THE COMMONWEALTH—1649 TO 1660

As none of the people either in England, Scotland, or Ireland, had expected King Charles would be put to death, you may suppose, my dear little Arthur, how angry many of them were when they heard what had happened.

In Ireland the Roman Catholics knew they should be treated worse by the Puritans than they had been by the king's governors and the English settlers expected to be no better used than the old Irish ; so they all made ready to fight against the army of the English parliament, if it should be sent to Ireland.

In Scotland, those who had sold King Charles to the English parliament were so angry with the English Round-heads for killing him that they chose Prince Charles, the son of the poor dead king, to be his successor ; and they got an army together to defend him and his friends.

As for England, the parliament (or rather the part of it that remained after the king's death) chose a number of persons to govern the kingdom, and called them a council of state ; and this council began to try to settle all those things quietly that had been disturbed by the sad civil war.

But the civil war in Ireland became so violent that the Council sent Oliver Cromwell, who was the best general in England, to that country ; and he soon won a good many battles, and made a great part of the country submit to the English. And he put his own soldiers into the towns, to keep them. As to the Irish who would have taken young King Charles' part, and were Roman Catholics, he sent many of them abroad, and treated others so hardly that they were glad to get out of the country. So Cromwell made Ireland quiet by force, and left General Ireton to take care of it.

While Cromwell was in Ireland a very brave Scotsman, whose name was James Graham, Marquis of Montrose, had gone to Scotland with soldiers from Germany and France, partly, as he said, to punish those who had allowed Charles the First to be beheaded, and partly to try to make Prince Charles king. This brave gentleman, whose story you will love to read some day, was taken prisoner by the Scottish army. The officers behaved very ill, for they forgot his bravery, and the kindness he had always shown to everybody when he was powerful. They forgot that he thought he was doing his duty in fighting for his king, and they put him to death very cruelly. They tied him to a cart, and dragged him disgracefully to prison. They hanged him on a tall gallows, with a book, in which his life was written, tied to his neck ; then they cut off his head and stuck it up over his prison-door.

About a month after the Scots had disgraced themselves by that cruel action, young Prince Charles, whom they called Charles the Second, arrived in Scotland. But he found that he was treated more like a prisoner than a king. The lords and generals of the Scottish army wanted him to be a presbyterian like them, but he liked better to go with the Scottish army into England, to try and persuade the English to fight for him, and to make him king.

But Cromwell, who had returned from Ireland, collected a large army in England, with which he marched into Scotland, and, finding that Charles meant to make war in

England, he followed him back again with part of the army, and left General Monk in Scotland with the rest.

Cromwell found King Charles and his army at Worcester, and there he fought and won a great battle, in which a great many Scottish noblemen were killed, as well as several English gentlemen. Charles was obliged to run away and hide himself, and for this time he gave up all hopes of being really King of England.

You would like, I daresay, to hear how he contrived to escape from Cromwell, who would certainly have shut him up in prison if he had caught him.

I must tell you that the English generals had promised a great deal of money to anybody who would catch Charles and bring him to them ; and they threatened to hang anybody who helped the poor young prince in any way ; but there were some brave men and women too, who had pity on him, as you shall hear.

After the battle of Worcester, the first place he got to was a farm called Boscobel, where some poor wood-cutters, of the name of Penderell, took care of him, and gave him some of their own clothes to wear, that the soldiers might not find out that he was the prince. One evening he was obliged to climb up into an oak tree, and sit all night among the branches ; it was well for him that the leaves were thick, for he heard some soldiers who were looking for him say, as they passed under the tree, that they were sure he was somewhere thereabouts.

At that time his poor feet were so hurt with going without shoes, that he was obliged to get on horseback to move to another place, where the good wood-cutters still went with him. This time he was hidden by a lady, who called him her servant, and made him ride with her, in woman's dress, to

Bristol, where she was in hopes that she should find a ship to take him to France. But there was no ship ready to sail. Then he went to a Colonel Windham's house, where the colonel, his mother, his wife, and four servants, all knew him ; but not one told he was there. At last he got a vessel to take him at Shoreham, in Sussex, after he had been in danger more times than I can tell you. He got safely to France, and did not come back to England for many years.

While Cromwell was following Charles to England, General Monk conquered the Scottish army, so that England, Scotland, and Ireland were all made obedient to the parliament about the time when the young king was driven out of the country.

But the parliament was obliged to attend to a war with the Dutch, who had behaved so very cruelly to some English people in India, that all England was eager to have them punished.

Accordingly the English and Dutch went to war, but they fought entirely on the sea. The Dutch had a very famous admiral named Tromp. The best English admiral was Blake, and these two brave men fought a great many battles. Tromp gained one or two victories ; but Blake beat him often ; and at last, on Tromp being killed, the Dutch were glad to make peace, and promised to punish all those persons who had behaved ill to the English in India, and to pay a great deal of money for the mischief they had done.

About four years after the death of King Charles the First, the officers of the army thought themselves strong enough to govern the kingdom without the parliament ; so one day Cromwell took a party of soldiers into the parliament-house, and turned everybody out, after abusing them heartily, and then locked up the doors. After this unlawful act, he soon

8*

contrived to get the people to call him the Protector of England, which was only another name for king, and from that time till his death he governed England as if he had been a lawful king.

Cromwell turns out the Parliament.

Cromwell was very clever, and always chose the best generals and admirals, whenever he sent armies or fleets to fight. He knew how to find out the very best judges to take care of the laws, and the wisest and properest men to send to foreign countries, when messages for the good or the honour of England were required. He rewarded those who served the country well, but he spent very little money on himself or his family. He treated the children of Charles that had not fled away to France with kindness. The little Princess Elizabeth and the Duke of Gloucester were allowed to live together at Carisbrook ; and a tutor and attendants were appointed to teach them and watch over them. The little princess soon died ; and then the young Duke was sent to France to his mother, and money was given him to pay the expenses of his journey.

After such a dreadful civil war as had made England unhappy during the reign of Charles I., the peace which was in the land, after Cromwell was made Protector, gave the people time to recover. Scotland was better governed than it had ever been before. Only poor turbulent Ireland was kept quiet by such means as made everything worse than before.

In foreign countries the name of England was feared more in Cromwell's time than it had ever been since the days of Henry V. And I must say of him that he used his power well.

He died when he had been Protector hardly five years.

There were a number of great men in the times of the civil wars. But I will only tell you of one, whom I have not named yet. He was Latin secretary to the Council of State, and to Cromwell. But what we best know him by, and love him for now, is his poetry. His name was John Milton ; and every Englishman must be proud that he was born in the same land, and that he speaks the same tongue with JOHN MILTON.

CHAPTER LI

CHARLES II.—1660 TO 1685

After Cromwell's death his friends wished his son, Richard Cromwell, to be Protector of England. But Richard, who was a shy, quiet man, did not like it, and after a very short trial went home to his house in the country, and left the people to do as they pleased about a Protector.

But the people were tired of being governed by the army, even under such a wise and considerate man as Cromwell, and they chose to have a king and a real parliament again.

Most men were glad to have bishops again, and to be allowed to have their own prayer-books and their own music in church, instead of being forced to listen for hours together to sermons from the Puritans, who called most pleasant things sinful, and grudged even little children their play-hours.

But the really wise people of all kinds, the English Protestants, the Puritans, and the Roman Catholics, had another reason for being glad the king was come home. I will try to explain this reason. You have read that whenever there was any dispute about who should be king, there was always a war of some kind, and generally the worst of all, a civil war. Now, if the people had to choose who should be their new king every time an old one died, so many men would wish to be king, that there would be disputes, and then perhaps war ; and while the war was going on there would be nobody to see that the laws were obeyed, and all the mischief would happen that comes in civil wars.

Now in England, it is settled that when a king dies his eldest son shall be king next ; or if he has no son, that his nearest relation shall be king or queen. You remember that after Edward the Sixth, his sisters, Mary and Elizabeth, were queens, and then their cousin, James Stuart, was king. This rule prevents all disputes, and keeps the kingdom quiet.

After Oliver Cromwell died, the wisest people were afraid there would be war before another protector could be chosen, so they agreed to have Charles, the son of Charles the First, for their king, and to get him to promise not to break the laws, or to oppress the people ; and they thought they would watch him, to prevent his doing wrong to the country, and they hoped he might have a son to be king quietly after him.

General Monk, who had the care of all Scotland in Cromwell's time, was the person who contrived all the plans for bringing Charles the Second to England. It was done very quietly. An English fleet went to Scheveling, in Holland, where Charles got on board, and he landed at Dover : in a very short time he arrived in London, along with General Monk, on his birth-day, the 29th of May, and England has never been without a king or queen since.

Charles was a merry, cheerful man, and very good natured. He was fond of balls, and plays, and masques, and nobody could have thought that England was the same place, who had seen it in Cromwell's time. Then, people wore plain black or brown clothes, stiff starched cravats or small collars, their hair combed straight down, and they all looked as grave as if they were walking to a funeral.

But when Charles came, the ladies and gentlemen put on

gay-coloured silk and satin coats ; they wore ribbons and
feathers, and long curly wigs, and danced and sang as if they
were at a wedding.

However, while Charles and the young men were so gay,

King Charles II. enters London at his Restoration.

there were a few old wise lawyers, and clergymen, and
admirals, and generals, who managed the laws and other
business very well, although there were a good many people
who were sadly vexed to see a king again in England.

The king soon married the Princess Catherine of Portugal, and her father gave her the island of Bombay, in the East Indies, as a wedding gift. It was almost the first place the English had in India, and now we have gained nearly all that large country, which is larger than England, and France, and Portugal, all put together.

While Charles the Second was king, there was a war with Holland, and another short one with France. Our battles with Holland were chiefly fought at sea : one of our best admirals was James, Duke of York, the king's brother, who beat the Dutch admirals, Opdam and the son of the famous Tromp. In another great battle, which lasted four days, General Monk, whom the king had made Duke of Albemarle, beat the great Admiral de Ruyter, and other English officers took several good towns which the Dutch had built in North America, especially New York.

Pleased with these victories, the king grew careless, and forgot to have the Dutch fleets properly watched, so one of them sailed into the river Medway, and burnt a number of English ships at Chatham, and did more mischief by landing at different places, and burning ships and houses, than had ever been done in the same way since the days of the old Danes.

This was near the end of the war. The English, Dutch, and French were equally glad to make peace.

The plague now broke out, first in Holland, then in England. Hundreds of people died every day, and it seemed shocking to be killing more men when so many were dying of that dreadful disorder.

Often when people did not know they had the plague they dropped down dead in the streets. Sometimes a friend would be talking to another and seem quite well and merry, and in a minute he would feel sick, and die before he could get

home. Sometimes everybody in a house would die, and
then the grave diggers had to go and get the dead out of the
house, and put them in a cart at night, and carry them to a
place near London, where a great grave was dug, so big that
many hundred people were buried there together. Sometimes a poor mother would follow the dead-cart crying,
because all her children were in it, and she had nobody left
alive to love. And often little children were found almost
starved, because their fathers and mothers were dead and there
was nobody to feed them. There was one lady whose name
was North, who had a very little baby ; that baby caught
the plague. The mother sent all her other children, and her
servants, and everybody else into the country, and stayed by
herself with the baby and nursed him, and would not fear
the plague while she was watching her sick child ; and it
pleased God to save her and the child too. I have read what
he says of his dear mother's love to him, in a book he wrote
when he was an oldish man ; and I think that the love he
always kept for his mother, and the remembrance of her kindness, made him a good man all his life.

This sad plague was put an end to by a dreadful fire, which
burnt down a great part of London. It lasted for four days ;
and though everybody tried to put an end to it, it still burned
on, for there was a strong wind, which blew the flames from
one house to another. At that time the streets were very
narrow, and most of the houses were built of wood, so no
wonder they burned fiercely.

But good arose from this evil : when London was built
again the streets were made wider, and the houses were built
of brick and stone, so they were not so apt to burn, and they
could be kept cleaner ; and as the plague seldom comes to
clean places, it has never been in London since the fire.

But now we must think about the king. Though he was a very merry man, he was far from being a good one. In the first part of his reign he listened to good advice, especially that given to him by Lord Clarendon, who had stayed with him all the time he was unhappy and poor, and while he was forced to live out of England. But it was not long before he neglected all the good and old friends of his father or of the people, and began to keep company with a number of gay men, who were always laughing and making jokes when they were seen ; but they gave the king bad advice in secret, and when they were trusted by him they behaved so ill to the people, that if it had not been for fear of another civil war, they would have tried to send Charles out of England again.

The Duke of Lauderdale, one of Charles's greatest friends, was sent to Scotland to govern it for Charles. Perhaps there never was so cruel and wicked a governor anywhere before. He ordered everybody to use the English prayer-book, and to leave off their own ways of worshipping God, and to change their prayers. And when he found any persons who did not, he had them shot or hanged at their own doors; and what was worse, if anybody would not tell where the people he wanted to shoot or to hang were to be found, he would put them in prison, or torture them by putting their legs in wooden cases, and then hammering them so tight that the bones were broken ; and this he did to children for saving their fathers and mothers, or to grown people for saving their children, or brothers, or sisters. I am sorry to say that another Scotsman, John Graham of Claverhouse, was his helper in all this wickedness.

Scotland was therefore very miserable under Charles, and you will read in larger histories that the Scots rebelled, and fought against the king.

Ireland was treated, if possible, worse ; and as to England, several parts were ready to rebel, especially when it came to be known that Charles and his four chief friends were so mean as to take money from the King of France to pay Charles for letting him conquer several other countries that England ought to have saved from him.

The king's brother, James, Duke of York, was known to approve of all the king's cruel and wicked actions ; so that the English people found, after all they had suffered in hopes of getting back their freedom, that Charles the Second wished as much to take it away as his father and grandfather did.

I do not wonder, therefore, that some wise, and good, and clever men, who loved our dear England as they ought to do, met together to talk about the best means of having proper parliaments again, and preventing the king from treating England, Scotland, and Ireland, so harshly.

One of these good men was William Lord Russell ; and another was Algernon Sidney. The king and his wicked friends found out that they were considering how to save the country from the bad government of Charles and James. They took Lord Russell and Algernon Sidney, and put them in prison, and shortly after condemned them to have their heads cut off.

Lord Russell's wife was one of the best women I ever read about. She went and knelt down at Charles's feet to beg him to spare her husband. She even tried to save him by offering a great deal of money to the greedy king ; but he would not save Lord Russell, and when Lady Russell found her dear husband must die, she attended him like his servant, she wrote for him like a clerk, she comforted him as none but a good wife can comfort a great man in his misfortunes ; and after his death she brought up his children to know his goodness

and try to be like him. The man who attended most to Lord
and Lady Russell at that time was Bishop Burnet, who has
written a true history of those things. He tells us that after
Lord Russell had taken leave of his wife, he said, " The
bitterness of death is past." Lord Cavendish, a friend of Lord
Russell's, offered to save him by changing clothes with him,
but Lord Russell refused, lest his friend should be punished
for saving him. He behaved as an Englishman ought to do
at his death, with courage, with gentleness to those people
who were with him, even to the man who was to cut off his
head, and with meekness and piety to God.

Algernon Sidney, who, though he wished for freedom,
took money from the King of France, was the next man put
to death by King Charles, and after him a great many who
were either his friends or Lord Russell's.

Soon after that Charles died and was not greatly mourned.
As I told you, his people were ready to love him when he
first came to be king ; but his extravagance and selfishness
soon changed their love into dislike.

CHAPTER LII

JAMES II.—1685 TO 1688

The reign of James the Second was a very short one, but many things were done in it which we must remember. You know that he was son of King Charles the First, who sent him to his mother in France to be taken care of during the civil war. This was bad for James, who was taught in France to be a Roman Catholic, to hate the English parliaments, and to think that kings might do as they chose, and change the religion of the country they governed, or take money, or put men in prison, without thinking whether it was just or unjust.

James married, first, a daughter of that Lord Clarendon who would have given good advice to Charles the Second, as I told you ; but neither Charles nor James would listen to him. James had two daughters when he came to be king ; they were both married ; the eldest to William, Prince of Orange, who was the king's nephew, and the second to Prince George of Denmark. You will hear more of both these ladies by and by. King James's second wife was an Italian lady, a princess of Modena, a Roman Catholic, proud and haughty, and disliked by the English.

Before James had been king a year, the Duke of Monmouth, who was his nephew, landed in England with a small army, in hopes the people would make him king instead of James. But King James's soldiers soon put an end to Monmouth's army, and the young Duke was sent to London where his head was cut off.

The king sent two men to punish the rebels in the parts where Monmouth's army was destroyed, Colonel Kirke and Judge Jeffries. These two men, by the king's orders, committed the greatest cruelties; they hung some men on different church steeples; some they cut to pieces before they were quite dead. A kind and charitable old woman, Mrs. Gaunt, was burnt alive because she had once given shelter to a conspirator against King Charles; and Lady Lisle was put to death for the same reason. In short, King James soon showed that he was as cruel and wicked as any king that ever reigned in any country, and the people began to hate him.

The next things that made the English people wish to get rid of James as a king, were his trying to govern without a parliament; his trying to give all power in Church and State to the Roman Catholics; and his putting seven English bishops in prison because they entreated him not to make the clergy read in church during divine service an unlawful proclamation.

The king ordered the bishops to be tried, in hopes that the judges would condemn them to be punished; but the jury (which is, you know, made up of twelve or more men, appointed to help the judge to find out the TRUTH) said that the bishops were not guilty of anything for which the king could punish them; and as soon as the people heard this, all those who were in the street waiting to hear what the judges would say, and even the king's own soldiers, set up such a shout for joy that the king heard it.

Instead of beginning a civil war, however, a number of the wisest and best English noblemen sent messages to William, Prince of Orange, who had married King James's eldest daughter, Mary, and invited him to come and help them to put an end to James's misrule and tyranny.

They asked William to come because he was a good Protestant, and the nearest relation to the king, next to his little son who was just born. Besides, William was a very brave prince, and had defended his own country against that grasping man, Louis the Fourteenth, King of France, who called himself Great because his army had won a great many battles and killed thousands of people.

William and Mary agreed to govern always by means of the parliament ; to do equal justice to all their subjects ; to listen to their complaints ; and never to let the Pope have anything to do with the government of England.

When these things were agreed to, William came over to England with a great many ships, and a large army, and began to march from Torbay, where he landed, to London. In a few days the gentlemen and people, and most of the noblemen of England joined him. Even the king's second daughter, the Princess Anne, with her husband, Prince George of Denmark, left King James, who found that he had hardly one friend in the world, no, not even his own children. The queen was hated even more than the king, so she made haste to run away, and the king put her, and a little baby boy that they had, into the care of a French nobleman, named Lauzun, who carried them to France, where King Louis received them kindly.

King James stayed a few days longer in England, in hopes to find some friends. But he had behaved too ill ; no Englishman would take his part. So in less than four years from the time he became King of England he was obliged to leave it for ever, and William, Prince of Orange, was made king by the whole people. And Mary was made queen, to reign with him, not like a queen who is only called so because she is the king's wife.

CHAPTER LIII

WILLIAM III. AND MARY II.—1688 TO 1702

The beginning of King William and Queen Mary's reign was very full of trouble.

It was some time before the parliament could put right many of the things that had been so wrong while James the Second was king ; and before everybody would agree how much money to give the king to spend upon the soldiers and sailors he might want in war, as well as upon judges and other persons whose duty it was to help the king to govern in peace as well as war.

Besides this, a great many people in Scotland liked James well enough to wish him to be their king still, because his grandfather came from Scotland ; and there were great disputes about allowing William to be king there. Lord Dundee, that Claverhouse who behaved so cruelly to the people in the time of Charles the Second, began a civil war against the new king ; but he was killed at the battle of Killiecrankie, in the Highlands of Scotland ; and, after a great deal of difficulty, William ruled as King of Scotland.

But William had more trouble with Ireland, as you shall read. When King James ran away from England he went to France, where his queen and little son were. Louis, King of France, who hated King William because he had always defended the countries and the people that Louis wanted to oppress, gave King James a good deal of money and many soldiers, and ships to carry them to Ireland, where he landed with them, and where most of the Irish under Lord Tyrconnel joined him, as well as many of the old English settlers, who were all Roman Catholics, and who did not wish for a Protestant king.

As soon as King William had settled the government in England he went to Ireland, where he found all the country distressed with civil war. King James with his army, made up of French, Irish, and English, was on one side of a river called the Boyne ; and there King William attacked his army, and beat it ; James stayed on the field watching the battle and giving advice until he saw the battle was lost ; and then, taking the advice of his general, Lauzun, he fled away with the French guards, and went back to France.

After this King James had no hope of gaining anything by fighting in Ireland ; but Ireland itself was much worse for a long while, for long years of quarrel began there at that time.

To the Protestants, who wished to have King William for their king, was given all the power in the country. They called themselves Orangemen because William was Prince of Orange ; and made many harsh laws against the Roman Catholics. For many years after this they tried very hard to get the rest of the Irish to turn Protestants ; and even now the Irish have not done disputing ; but I hope before many more years have gone past that all the Irish will be friends, and live in peace, not only among themselves but with England too. It is dreadful to think that, though it is many more than two hundred years since the battle of the Boyne, Ireland has been unhappy all that time. Sometimes one side, sometimes the other, has been cruel and revengeful ; but now the Irish enjoy the same freedom as the English, and we must hope in future they will put aside their old angers and grievances and see that it is best for them, as it is for us, in all ways to be friendly with and loyal to the Empire of which they and we are equal members. Of this Empire or Commonwealth I must tell you something later.

While King William was busy in Ireland, Queen Mary governed in England, and, by her gentle and kind behaviour to everybody, gained the love of the people ; so that they were glad to have her to govern, whenever William was obliged to go to Holland, to carry on the war which had been begun by several countries, as well as England, against that proud and ambitious king, Louis the Fourteenth of France. Louis was one of those strange men who fancy that they are born better than others, and that people have nothing to do but to obey them, and that every man and every country must be wicked that does not do exactly as they choose in every thing, even in the way of worshipping God.

Now King William knew that kings are only to be better loved and obeyed than other men when they obey God themselves, and love mercy, and do right and justice to their subjects ; and that men and countries have a right to be free, and to worship God as they please : and it was because King William knew this that the English chose him to be king when they sent away James the Second, because he wished to be like Louis the Fourteenth in most things.

The war the French king had begun went on for a good many years. Twice people made a plot to murder King William, but they were found out and punished, and the people in England were so angry at such wicked plans, that they gave William more money to pay soldiers and sailors for the war than they had ever given to any king before.

Our king used to go every spring, as long as the war lasted, to fight the French on the borders of France, and he came home in the autumn to see what had been done in England while he was away.

The bravest admiral in these times was Admiral Russell, who beat the French ships whenever he could find them, and who fought a very famous battle against the French Admiral Tourville, about which those who love the English sailors sing some fine songs even now.

King William himself was so brave and skilful in war that he baffled the best French generals, and kept King Louis' large armies from getting any decisive advantage for many years, till at last Louis was tired of war, and was glad to make peace. So he sent his ambassadors to a place called Ryswick, in Holland, where King William had a country-house, and promised to give back all the places he had taken from his neighbours during the war, provided he might have peace.

But in the midst of the war, when everything seemed to be going on well, a great misfortune happened to both the king and people of England. Good Queen Mary died of the small-pox when she had been queen only six years. She was a very good and clever woman. She was not only a good wife to the king, but his best friend ; and he trusted her, and took her advice in everything. She was a true Protestant and very religious, which made her particularly fit to be Queen of England. She was a cheerful, good-tempered woman, which made the people love her ; and the ladies who lived at her court were good wives and mothers, and spent part of their time in useful work and reading, like the queen, instead of being always at plays, or gaming, or dressing, as they used to be in the time of Charles and James.

King William lived seven years after the queen died. He was killed by a fall from his horse near Hampton Court.

He was not nearly so pleasant and cheerful as Queen Mary

But he was the best king for England that we could have found at that time.

He was a religious man, and he knew his duty, and loved to do it, both in England, where the people chose him for their king, and in Holland, his own country.

I must write down a few of the things that he did for England : perhaps you will not quite understand how right they were till you are older, but it is proper that you should remember them.

A law was made that no man or woman should ever be king or queen of England but a Protestant.

It was settled that there should be a new parliament very often, and that no year should pass without the meeting of a parliament.

The old money that had been used in England was so worn out, and there was so much bad among it, that the king ordered it to be coined, or made over again, of a proper size and weight, so that people might buy and sell with it conveniently.

A number of merchants agreed to call themselves the East India Company, and to pay a tax to the king and parliament, if the king would protect them, and not allow any nation with which England was at war to hurt or destroy the towns in India where they had their trade, or their ships when they were carrying goods from place to place. There was a small company of this kind in Queen Elizabeth's reign, but the new one in William's time was of more use to the country as well as to the merchants.

We call the East India trade, not only the trade in things from India itself, such as pepper, cotton, muslin, diamonds, and other things that come from that country, but the trade in tea, and silk, and nankeen, and ivory, from China ; and in spice of many kinds from the Spice Islands ; and cinnamon and gold, and precious stones, and many kinds of medicine from Ceylon. And all this trade came to be very great in King William's reign.

The reign of King William will always be thought of gratefully by good Englishmen ; because then the best things were done for the government, the religion, the laws, and the trade of our dear England.

CHAPTER LIV

QUEEN ANNE—1702 TO 1714

The Princess Anne, who was the second daughter of King James the Second, and sister to King William's wife Mary, became Queen of England when King William died, because she had been brought up a Protestant; while her little brother was taught to be a Roman Catholic; so that by law he could never be king of England. He is commonly called the Pretender, and he and his son often gave trouble in England, as you will read by and by.

The first ten years of Queen Anne's reign were glorious; but the last part of her life was troubled by the quarrels of some of the great men who wished to be her favourites, and to direct her affairs.

We will begin her history, however, with the most useful thing that was done in her reign; and that is, the union of Scotland with England.

You know that when Queen Elizabeth died, her cousin, James, king of Scotland, became king of England, so both countries had one king; but, as they had separate parliaments, and different ministers, and a different form of religion, they were always quarrelling, and many disputes, and even battles, took place, which were as bad as civil wars. These disputes were often on account of religion, because the king and his counsellors in England wanted to force the Scots to worship God in the same way, using the same words with the English. This was very unjust; so a great many Scotsmen joined

together, and made a COVENANT, or agreement, to preserv
their own way of worship, even if they should be obliged t
fight for it.

I told you that in William's reign it was settled by law tha
the Scotch should do as they chose about their religion ; an
that wise king saw that it would be better for both nation
if they could be so united as to have but one parliament ; an
if he had lived longer, he meant to make this union. Afte
his death Queen Anne and her friends desired the same thing
but it was several years before the Scottish and English peop
would agree to it. At last, however, it was settled ; and no
the Scottish must wonder that they ever thought it a ba
thing. Since that time they have been equal in everythin
with England. They keep their own religion and laws,
well as the English ; and when new laws are made, they a
contrived to be fit for both countries ; or, if they will on
suit one, then they are made on purpose for the people in th
one. As there are plenty of Scottish lords and gentlemen,
well as English, in the parliament, they are always ready
take care of their own country, which is right.

Although Queen Anne and her ministers were busy abo
this union of Scotland with England, they were obliged
attend to what the French, under their ambitious king, Lou
the Fourteenth, were about. They had begun to attack t
Protestants again, in so many ways, before King Willia
died, that there was likely to be a war ; and now he was dea
Louis thought there was no country in Europe strong enoug
or with a soldier good enough, to fight him, or prevent
conquering as many countries as he pleased. But he was mi
taken. The English were as much determined in Que
Anne's time as in King William's to prevent Louis fro
forcing upon them a Popish king and from oppressing t

Protestants ; and Queen Anne possessed in the great Duke of Marlborough a far more skilful general than William had ever been. Indeed King William in the last year of his life intended to give him the command of the whole army, for he thought he should be too ill to command it himself. The English had a great many fine ships too, and Queen Anne's husband, Prince George of Denmark, was admiral. So England was quite ready for war against King Louis, and the people and parliament were ready to give the queen all the money she wanted to pay the soldiers and sailors.

Besides this, the Dutch were glad to fight on our side, as well as some of the princes in Germany ; and another firm ally of the English was Prince Eugene of Savoy, who was Queen Anne's cousin, and was almost as good a general as the Duke of Marlborough.

When Anne had been queen about two years, the greatest battle that had ever been heard of was fought at a place called Blenheim, near the village of Hochstet, in Germany, between the English and French. The English had the Dutch and an army of Germans on their side ; their generals were Marlborough and Prince Eugene. The French had a good many Germans and Spaniards and Italians with them ; their generals were Marshals Marsin and Tallard, and the Elector of Bavaria.

The English had to march through a little brook to attack the French, who stood very steady for a little while ; but so many were killed, that the rest began to run away. Some were drowned in the river Danube, which was very near them, and a great many were taken prisoners, with their general, Tallard, amongst them. The fighting lasted six hours on a very hot day. A cannon-ball very nearly hit the Duke of Marlborough just as the fight began : it struck the earth so close to him that the cloud of dust it sent up hid him

for some minutes from the sight of the people about him
The English and Dutch and Germans took all the guns, and
money, and food of the French army, besides a very grea
number of prisoners. There were more than twelve thousan

Marlborough at Blenheim.

French killed, and a great many wounded; and about ha
as many English and Dutch and Germans.

So you see that, whichever side wins in a great battle, the
is sure to be misery for many families on both, who have t

grieve for their fathers, and sons, and brothers, killed or hurt.

This was a good battle, however, for it saved many countries from the cruel government which Louis the Fourteenth set up wherever he conquered.

Nearly at the same time with the battle of Blenheim, a place called Gibraltar was taken by the English Admiral Rooke, which is of great use to England.

If you look at the map of Europe, you will see that where the Mediterranean Sea joins the great Atlantic Ocean, Gibraltar is placed. Now all captains of ships who want to go into the Mediterranean must pass that way. You would be surprised if you could see the number of ships of all sizes that pass there every day. They fetch figs, and currants, and silk, and fine wool, and shawls, and velvets, and wine, and oil, and a great many other useful things from the Mediterranean; and whoever Gibraltar belongs to can stop the ships going in and out. So the English were very glad that Admiral Rooke took Gibraltar for Queen Anne.

At last, after Marlborough had gained several other battles, peace was made with the French at a place called Utrecht, and Queen Anne died the very next year.

Queen Anne was kind and good-natured, but not very clever. She was rather lazy, and allowed the Duchess of Marlborough to govern her for several years. Afterwards she quarrelled with her, and then some other ladies governed her.

In the reign of Queen Anne there were a great many clever men in England, some poets, and many writers of other things. Pope was the great poet, and Addison wrote beautiful prose. But our little history would not hold an account of half of them.

9

Queen Anne's husband and all her children died before her, and though she did not love any of her Protestant cousins, it was settled by law that the son of her cousin Sophia, who was married to the Elector of Hanover, should be king after her.

CHAPTER LV

GEORGE I.—1714 TO 1727

George the First was Elector of Hanover, in Germany ; and as it was settled in King William's reign that nobody but a Protestant should be king of England, he was sent for and made king of England, rather than the son of James the Second, who was a Roman Catholic.

But a great many people in Scotland still wished to have a king of the old Scottish family of Stuart again ; so they encouraged young James Stuart, that is the Pretender, whom they called King James, to come to Scotland, and promised they would collect men and money enough to make an army, and buy guns and everything fit for soldiers, and march into England, and make him king instead of George the First. From this time all those who took the part of the Pretender against George were called Jacobites, from Jacobus, the Latin for the Pretender's name, James.

James's chief friend in Scotland was Lord Mar, and he was in hopes that a great many English gentlemen would join him, and send money from England, and get another army ready there to help him.

But the Pretender and his friends were disappointed. They lost a great many men in battle at the Sheriffmuir, near Dunblane, in Perthshire. Their English army was beaten at Preston in Lancashire, and the Pretender was obliged to get away as fast as he could to France again.

I wish King George had forgiven both the Jacobite officers

and men, who thought they were doing right in fighting for
the son of their old king : but he would not ; and besides
putting to death a few common soldiers and gentlemen, he
ordered six lords to have their heads cut off. One of them
escaped, however, and three were afterwards pardoned.
Lord Nithisdale, who escaped, was saved by the devotion and
courage of his wife. She had tried by every means to prevail
upon the king to pardon him, but he would not ; however,
she had leave to visit him in prison. She went, you may be
sure, often, and she took a friend with her, whom she called
her maid, till she had used the jailers to see two people go in
and out. Then she made her friend put on double clothes
one day, and as soon as she got into Lord Nithisdale's room
half those clothes were taken off, and he was dressed in them,
and so they managed that he should go out with one of the
ladies, who pretended that her companion had so bad a tooth-
ache that she could not speak. Lady Nithisdale had a coach
waiting at the prison-door, and they went to a safe place,
where her husband was hidden till he could get to France.

And this was the end of the first civil war begun in Scotland for the sake of the Pretender. Although his friends often
tried to begin another, they always failed, while George the
First was king.

The King of Spain also tried to assist the Pretender, but he
could only make war with England by sea, and his ships were
always beaten ; and so he made peace.

George the First died while he was visiting his own country
of Hanover, after he had been King of England thirteen years.
He was a brave and prudent man, but was too old, when he
came to be King of England, to learn English, or to behave
quite like an Englishman. Yet still, upon the whole, he was
a useful king.

CHAPTER LVI

GEORGE II.—1727 TO 1760

The reign of George the Second was disturbed both by foreign and civil war, and by some disputes in his family at home. His eldest son, Frederick, Prince of Wales, married a German princess, and they both lived in London, but they were discontented with the money the king gave them to spend, so they quarrelled with him, and he ordered them to go and live at Kew, and would not do anything kind or good-natured for them. Two children were born to them, one of whom was afterwards King George the Third, but the Prince of Wales died before his father.

I will now tell you about King George's foreign wars, and keep the story of the civil war to the last for you, because you will like it best, I think.

The Spaniards had built a great many towns in South America ; and after they had got possession of the country, and killed many of the people, they took all the gold and silver that was found in the earth there for themselves. They were therefore obliged to have a great many ships to fetch it, and brave soldiers and sailors to guard it as it crossed the seas, and so Spain got more gold and silver than any other country.

But other countries wished for some of the useful things from South America too ; and some English merchants wished very much to have several kinds of wood which are useful for dyeing cloth and wool and other things of different colours ; but the Spaniards attacked them and ill-used them for trying to cut the wood, and behaved in other respects very ill, so England went to war with Spain.

The war was mostly by sea, and in the course of it the Spaniards were beaten, first by Admiral Vernon, and then by Admirals Hawke, Rowley, Warren, and particularly Anson, though they none of them did all they hoped to do.

Another admiral was very unfortunate. He had to fight a great many ships in the Mediterranean Sea, and because he did not do all that the people of England desired him to do, he was shot when he came to England. His name was Byng. I do not admire this admiral, but I think he was not justly treated.

Besides the Spaniards, George the Second was at war with the French and Bavarians. The Prince of Bavaria had been made Emperor, and tried to make himself King of Bohemia, in the room of the lawful queen, Maria Theresa, and her son, who was an infant. The English and Dutch took Maria Theresa's part, the French took that of the Prince of Bavaria, and there was a very fierce war on that account, in which the English gained some battles, and lost some others, an account of which would be very tiresome to you, I am sure.

Though upon the whole the French had rather the best of the war in Europe, Lord Clive, who had an army of English in the East Indies, to take care of our merchants and our towns there, beat the French generals, and almost drove the French from India altogether. Some time afterwards the French sent an army under Count Lally to win back their power in India ; but Lally was so beaten that the French have never had more than one or two small towns in that part of the world since.

If you look at the map of the world in this place, my dear little Arthur, you will wonder that two countries in Europe, so close together as England and France, should think of sending their soldiers and sailors so far off as India to fight their battles ; but you will wonder still more when you learn that, not content with this, they sent other fleets and armies to North America, where they fought till the English conquered the greatest part of all the country that the French ever had in that part of the world. But the greatest victory we gained there was the battle of Quebec, where our brave and good General Wolfe was killed. Some day you will read his life, and then you will wish that all English soldiers could be like him.

We will now think about the civil war in King George the Second's reign. You remember that in his father's time the Pretender, whom the Scots call James the Eighth, came from France to Scotland, and thought he could get the kingdom for himself, but he was soon obliged to go back again.

After that he went and lived in Italy, and married a Princess of Poland, and had two sons. The eldest of these was a fine brave young man : the youngest became a clergyman, and the Pope made him a Cardinal ; his name was Henry. The eldest, Charles Edward, who was called the Young Chevalier in Scotland and in England the Young Pretender, thought he would try once more to get the kingdom of Great Britain from the Protestant king ; so, in spite of the good advice of his true friends, he would go from Italy first to France, and then to Scotland, to make war against King George.

The King of France lent him a ship and a few men and officers, and gave him a little money, for this purpose ; and the young prince landed in Scotland, among the highlands, where the people were still fond of his family. In a very short time the highland chiefs, who had a great power over the poor people, gathered a great army, and marched to Edinburgh, which you know is the capital of Scotland.

There he had his father proclaimed King of England, Scotland, and Ireland, and gave titles of dukes and lords to the gentlemen who came to fight for him, and pretended to be the real Prince of Wales. And he lived in the old palace of the Scottish kings, called Holyrood House, and there he gave balls and concerts to the Scottish ladies, and they all fancied themselves sure that Charles Edward would be their king instead of George.

At first he gained two or three victories, the chief of which was at Preston Pans, near Edinburgh ; and then he marched into England, where but few English gentlemen joined him, and when he got as far as Derby he found that he had better go back to Scotland, for the English would have nothing to do with him. Finding no real encouragement in the south, it was decided, though much against the will of Prince Charlie, to retreat to the Highlands.

From this time the French and Scottish officers of the Pretender quarrelled constantly, and the highland chiefs became jealous of the other generals, and everything began to be unfortunate for that unhappy prince, till at the battle of Culloden his whole army was destroyed, many officers were taken prisoners, and he was obliged to make his escape and hide himself till he could get back to France.

Sometimes the young prince was obliged to go many days without any food but wild berries in the woods, and to sleep in caves, or on the open ground. Sometimes he lay in bed, pretending to be a sick man, while the Duke of Cumberland's soldiers were hunting for him, and he could hear them talking of him. Once he escaped from a great danger by being dressed in women's clothes, and seeming to be the maid-servant of a very kind and handsome young lady, called Flora MacDonald, who saved his life. At last he got safe away ;

and though he and his friends often threatened to make war
in England again, they never could do any real mischief; and
as he and his brother Henry both died without children, we
have had no more Pretenders.

The Pretender at Holyrood House.

I am sorry to say that the Duke of Cumberland was very
cruel to Prince Charles's friends when the war was over.
Three Scottish lords, a good many gentlemen, and a number
of soldiers, were executed for having joined the Pretender.

9*

There is nothing else to tell you about the reign of George the Second ; he was a very old man when he died at Kensington. He had fought many battles in Germany, and was a brave soldier, and not a bad king ; but having been brought up in Germany, like his father, he never either looked or talked like an English king.

CHAPTER LVII

GEORGE III.—1760 TO 1820

The people of England were glad when George the Third became king after his grandfather. You read in the last chapter that his father, Frederick, Prince of Wales, died in the life-time of George the Second.

George the Third was born in England, and brought up like an English gentleman. I think he was one of the best men that ever was a king ; but I do not think that everything he did was wise or right. He reigned longer than any king ever reigned in England, and unhappily before he died he became blind, and he lost his senses.

He married a German princess named Charlotte, and they had a great many sons and daughters, and one of their grand-children was our Queen Victoria.

You must not expect me to tell you everything that happened in this long reign, which lasted sixty years, but you shall read of one or two things of most consequence, and that you can understand best.

When George had been king a little more than two years, he made peace with all the world, but his reign was very far from being a peaceable one.

There were two wars in particular of great consequence ; the first was the American war, and the second the French war. I will tell you a little about each of them.

You will remember that in Raleigh's time the English built some towns in North America. Afterwards, during the civil wars in the time of Charles the First, many more English went there and took their families there to live, and by degrees they had taken possession of a very large country, and had got towns and villages, and fields. These English states in America were called *Colonies* ; but they were still governed by the King and parliament of England. The English wanted the Americans to pay taxes. But the Americans said that, by Magna Carta and our old laws, no Englishman might be taxed without their own consent given in parliament. Now the American Colonies had no members in the British parliament ; so they said the Parliament had no right to tax them. Then the king called them rebels, and threatened to punish them ; and so, after many disputes, war broke out between the Americans and the King of England's soldiers who were in America to guard the towns and collect the taxes. Then the Americans said they would have a government of their own. This war was thought little of at first, but it soon grew to be one of the greatest wars England had ever had. The French and Spaniards, who had not forgotten how the English had beaten them by sea and land in the last wars, joined the Americans ; and although the English gained several victories by sea over the French and the Spaniards, yet by land the Americans beat the English.

The chief man in America was General George Washington, one of the greatest men that ever lived. He commanded the American army, and as he and his soldiers were fighting in their own land for their own freedom, and for their own wives and children, it was not wonderful that at last they beat out the English soldiers, who did not like to be sent so far from home to fight against men who spoke the same language with themselves.

At last, when the King of England found the people were

tired of this long war, he agreed to make peace with America, and since that time the UNITED STATES OF AMERICA have had a government of their own, and have become a great and powerful nation. They have a President instead of a king, and they call their parliament a Congress. You will understand these things in a few years.

The French war lasted even longer than the American war. This was the cause : for a long time the French kings had governed France very badly, and the French nobles oppressed the poor people, and the clergymen did not do their duty rightly, but left the people ignorant. At last the people could bear these bad things no longer, and King Louis the Sixteenth, who wished to do well, would have made them better if he could. But the princes and nobles would not let him. Then the French Revolution broke out and caused much sorrow and cruelty. A number of bad people seized the government in Paris, and they put the king and queen and all their family in prison, and they cut off the heads of the king and queen and the king's sister, and of a great many lords and ladies, and killed many others ; in short, I believe the French people did more wicked things in about three years than any other nation had done in a hundred up to that time. The name of the most wicked of all was Robespierre ; he was killed at last by some of those he meant to kill.

England and several other countries then went to war with the French, because they had sent armies to attack the neighbouring countries, and had conquered many of them, and that war lasted about twenty-four years.

France would have been mastered, I think, if it had not been for a brave and clever but very ambitious man, called Napoleon Buonaparte, who, from being a simple lieutenant rose to be Emperor of the French. He chose able men for judges and generals. He conquered many countries, and used to threaten to come and conquer England. But we had brave sailors and clever captains and admirals, who never let any of his ships come near us. Lord Howe won the first sea victory in the war ; then we had Lord St. Vincent, Admirals Duncan, Hood, Collingwood, Cornwallis, Cochrane, Pellew, and many more, who gained battles at sea, besides more captains than I can tell you, who took parts of fleets or single ships. But the man that will be remembered for ever as the greatest English sailor was Admiral Lord NELSON. He gained three great victories—at Aboukir in Egypt, at Copenhagen, and at TRAFALGAR near the coast of Spain. In that battle he was killed, but he knew his own fleet had conquered before he died. When he went into battle, the words he gave to tell all the ships when to begin to fight, were, ENGLAND EXPECTS EVERY MAN WILL DO HIS DUTY.

These words must never be forgotten by any Englishman.

There were no more great sea fights after Trafalgar, but many on land, where we had good generals and brave soldiers. The wise and good General Abercromby was killed just as he had gained a victory in Egypt. His friend, the brave Sir John Moore, was killed at Corunna in Spain, and many other officers and men died for the sake of England, but many lived to fight and to conquer. The greatest general in that time was the Duke of WELLINGTON, who put an end to the sad long war by his great victory over the French, commanded by Napoleon himself, at WATERLOO. I cannot tell you in this little book how many other battles he won or how skilfully he fought them, or how well he knew how to choose the officers to help him. But he will have always a

name as great as Nelson, by whose side he was buried in St.
Paul's.

Farmhouse of Hougoumont on the Field of Waterloo.

After the battle of Waterloo, Napoleon Buonaparte was
kept a prisoner in the island of St. Helena till he died, and the

brother of Louis the Sixteenth was King of France, under the
title of Louis the Eighteenth.

Our good king, George the Third, died soon after. I have
told you what kind of man he was at the beginning of this
chapter.

In his reign more things, useful to all men, were found out
than in hundreds of years before. New countries were
visited, new plants and new animals were brought to England.
All the sciences received great encouragement. The arts that
are needful in common life were improved. Steam engines
were first made useful. The beautiful light given by gas was
found out, and all sorts of machines to assist men in their
labour were invented. Those arts called the fine arts, I mean
such as sculpture, painting, and music, were encouraged by
George the Third. But what is of more consequence, the
science of medicine and the art of surgery were so improved
in his time, that the sufferings of mankind from pain and
sickness are much lessened.*

* This is the end of little Arthur's History, as first written by Lady
Callcott; but for the benefit of the children of the present day who read
this little History, a few more chapters are added.

CHAPTER LVIII

GEORGE IV.—1820 TO 1830

When George the Fourth came to the throne, he was fifty-eight years old, but he had been governing the kingdom for eight years before he was king, during which time he had been called the Prince Regent. The reason of this was, that the old king, who, as you read in the last chapter, had the misfortune to go out of his mind, never quite recovered his reason from the time his youngest daughter, the Princess Amelia, died; so George, Prince of Wales, being the heir to the throne, governed for his father all that time.

George the Fourth had no sooner begun his reign than a dreadful plot was formed to kill all the cabinet ministers. The wicked men—about thirty, I believe—who contrived this plot, used to meet at a house in an out-of-the-way place called Cato Street, in London; and there they agreed to carry out their plan on a certain day, when the ministers were all expected to meet together and dine. Fortunately the plot was betrayed by one of the men, in time to prevent the murder: most of the conspirators were seized, and the leader Thistlewood and four others were hanged.

About twenty-five years before George the Fourth came to the throne, he had married his cousin, the Princess Caroline of Brunswick. The marriage was not a happy one, and the Prince and Princess of Wales separated soon after the birth of their first and only child, the Princess Charlotte. This led to a sad quarrel, which I think it is no use for us to remember.

The Princess Charlotte, who would have succeeded her father on the throne if she had survived him, had married Prince Leopold of Saxe-Coburg, but died the year after her marriage, to the great grief of the people. This happened before her father became king.

It was towards the middle of King George's reign that a war broke out between the Greeks and Turks. A great many English gentlemen, amongst whom was the poet, Lord Byron, went to Greece to take the part of the Greeks. The struggle lasted several years, and was ended by a battle fought in the harbour of Navarino, where all the Turkish ships were sunk by the British fleet—Navarino is at the south-west corner of the Morea in Greece. The commander of the Turkish fleet was named Ibrahim Pacha, and the commander of the English fleet was Sir Edward Codrington. After this battle, Greece, which had been subject to Turkey, was made into an independent kingdom, and three German princes were invited in turn to be king ; Prince Leopold of Saxe-Coburg (who had married our Princess Charlotte) declined, but Prince Otho of Bavaria accepted the invitation, and became Otho the First, King of Greece. Lord Byron died in Greece three years before the war ended. Otho was afterwards sent away because he governed badly, and the crown was given to Prince George of Denmark, who was brother to our Queen Alexandra.

A law was passed in this reign to allow Roman Catholics to sit in Parliament and help to make laws for the country. There was much talking and considering before this was done, for many people thought that if the Roman Catholics helped to make laws, they would try to change the religion of the country, and to bring back popery. Others, believing that the Roman Catholics of the present day were wiser, and that they would continue loyal to the Sovereign and faithful to the laws of the land, consented to admit them to equal privileges with their Protestant fellow-countrymen. So at last this law was passed; and now Roman Catholics sit in Parliament, and enjoy every right and privilege that other Britons have, except that of being the Lord Chancellor, who keeps the Great Seal and presides over the meetings of the House of Lords.

About the same time the severe laws against Protestant Dissenters, which were made under Charles the Second, were done away with.

The king died at Windsor at the age of sixty-eight, after a reign of ten years.

George the Fourth was an able man, but he cared so much more for pleasing himself than for doing his duty and thinking of others, that he was not a favourite with his people.

Many new buildings were erected and improvements made in this reign. The New London Bridge and the Thames Tunnel were begun; the Menai Suspension Bridge, joining the Isle of Anglesey to North Wales, was completed; the Regent's Park was laid out in London; the Zoological Gardens were opened; and Regent Street and other handsome streets were built.

One very great improvement was made by Sir Robert Peel in causing the streets and roads to be guarded night and day by active, well-drilled policemen, instead of by watchmen, who used to be on duty only at night, and who were very frequently feeble old men scarcely able to take care of themselves.

CHAPTER LIX

WILLIAM IV.—1830 to 1837

As King George the Fourth left no child to succeed him, his brothers were the next heirs to the throne. The Duke of York, the second son of George the Third, died three years before George the Fourth, and left no child; so William Henry, Duke of Clarence, the third son of George the Third, now mounted the throne. William the Fourth, who had been brought up as a sailor, was at this time sixty-four years old; he was married to an excellent German princess, named Adelaide of Saxe Meiningen, and he had had two daughters, but they both died in early infancy.

This reign was a short one, but several important changes took place in it, one of which was the passing of the Bill for a reform in the House of Commons. You know how it was settled by King Edward the First that all the large towns, which in his reign were called burghs, should choose one or two persons to go to Parliament and help to make the law. Since that time a great many little hamlets and villages had grown into large towns, and a great many of the old burghs had dwindled away until only a few houses were left in them, or even none. The people, who were now living in the towns that had grown so large, thought it very hard not to be able to send members to Parliament to tell what was wanted in their towns; and they also thought it was useless for the little burghs, where only a few people lived, to continue sending members. So it was proposed that the large towns or boroughs should be allowed to send members to the House of Commons, according to the number of people in each town, and that the little decayed towns should leave off sending members. This new plan was called the " Reform Bill." It was talked over a long time in Parliament before it was agreed to ; for, although there were a great many people who wished for the change, there were many others who thought it would be dangerous to the welfare of Old England, and both sides had to tell all their reasons for what they thought. At last it was put to the vote whether the Bill should pass or not ; and as the greatest number were for making the change, the Bill became law. But I shall have to tell you of another Reform of Parliament under Queen Victoria.

Nearly the next thing that was done was to put an end to slavery in all the colonies belonging to England. A good man, named William Wilberforce, had tried to do this many years ago, in George the Third's reign ; but it was not an easy thing to do, because all those persons who had large estates in the colonies, and who had bought slaves to cultivate the land, had paid a great deal of money for their slaves ; and the masters were afraid they should be ruined if the slaves were set free, as there would be no one to sow and dig their fields.

There is no doubt the Parliament and people of England acted wisely in wiping away so great a disgrace as *slavery* is ; and in order to do this with justice they paid a very large sum of money—twenty millions of pounds. When this was at last done, the slaves were made free.

There was a very sudden revolution in France at the beginning of this reign. It only lasted three days, and was called the " Three Days' Revolution." Charles the Tenth, the King of France, was expelled, and came over to this country ; his cousin Louis Philippe was then chosen by the French people to be their king, and was called the King of the French.

The example of France was followed in Belgium, a country which had been joined to Holland, so as to make but one kingdom, over which the Dutch king reigned. The Belgians fought hard, and succeeded in driving away the Dutch ; after which they invited Prince Leopold of Saxe-Coburg to be their king. Although Prince Leopold would not be King of Greece, he accepted the kingdom of Belgium. He reigned a long time and wisely, and was succeeded by his son Leopold the Second.

I will now tell you of some improvements that were made in King William's reign, the principal of which is perhaps the forming of railways. The first that was opened in England was one between Liverpool and Manchester ; and it was a very useful one. You know that the people at Manchester weave great quantities of cotton, so much, indeed, that the town is full of factories, where thousands of spinners and weavers are at work. After the railway was opened, the work went on faster than ever, for as soon as the raw cotton arrived in bales from America to Liverpool, it was sent off by rail to Manchester ; and as fast as it was spun and woven at Manchester, a great deal was sent back by rail to Liverpool, to be shipped off to America, and other parts of the world. This kept a great many people at work, and as this railway seemed to do so much good, railways were very soon carried from one end of Britain to the other.

Amongst the sad events of this reign, may be mentioned the appearance of the cholera in England, and a great fire which destroyed the Houses of Parliament at Westminster.

William the Fourth died, after a reign of seven years, at the age of seventy-one ; and his widowed Queen Adelaide, who then became Queen Dowager, survived him about twelve years, when she died, much loved and respected by the English people.

CHAPTER LX

QUEEN VICTORIA—1837 TO 1901

William IV. was succeeded on the throne by his young niece, the Princess Victoria. She was the grand-daughter of George III., who, you remember, married a German princess. He had fifteen children, but only his fourth son, Edward, Duke of Kent, left a child to succeed to the throne of England.

Princess Victoria was just eighteen when she was called to be Queen of England. Her father died when she was quite a baby, and she had been very quietly brought up by her widowed mother at Kensington. Some day, perhaps, my dear Arthur, you will see the room in Kensington Palace, where this good and great Queen was born.

When the messengers came to tell her that her uncle the king, William IV., was dead, they found that she was fast asleep in bed, for it was yet early in the morning. It was important that she should hear the news at once, so they told her maid to awaken her. The girl appeared in her dressing-gown, with a shawl thrown over her shoulders ; she had slippers on her feet, and her hair fell loose. When told that she was no longer Princess Victoria but the Queen of England, tears rose to her eyes, as she thought of the great duties that lay before her.

But I am glad to be able to tell you, that it was a very happy day for England when she became Queen, for she ruled her country well and wisely for sixty-three years. She ruled longer than any king or queen had ever ruled before, except Louis XIV., who had ruled over France for seventy-one years. When she died, at the age of eighty-one, not only her own country, but the whole world mourned for her.

When she began to reign, there was peace everywhere. So the people at home had plenty of time to improve the railways and steamboats, which were coming into use. You remember that I told you of the first train that ever ran in England, carrying passengers from Liverpool to Manchester. This was a very short distance. Soon, lines were laid all over the land, and it was discovered that trains could go much faster than was at first supposed or had been thought to be safe. Five years after her accession, the Queen herself travelled by train for the first time from Windsor to London.

Up to this time, steamboats had only been used on the large rivers; but the year after the Queen came to the throne, a steamer crossed the Atlantic from Bristol to New York in fifteen days. The old sailing-boats had taken about a month to travel the same distance, so this was a great improvement.

You see, my dear Arthur, how much easier it was becoming to visit and send letters to other countries, and how this would help on England's trade and also, it was hoped, friendship between the different nations.

Another great help was the Penny Post. When Queen Victoria came to the throne, only rich people could send letters to one another, because the rates of postage were so very high. It cost one shilling and threepence to send a letter to a friend in Scotland, for letters had to be sent by coach over hundreds of miles, and only members of Parliament could send them free of cost. The postage then was fixed at a penny a letter, and that penny was paid, as you know, by

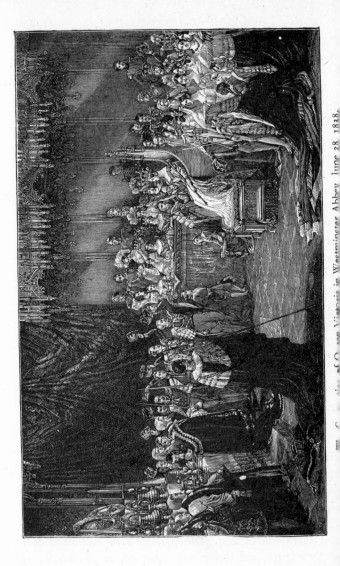

The Coronation of Queen Victoria in Westminster Abbey, June 28, 1838.

the purchase of a stamp bearing a picture of the young Queen's head.

A little later, the electric telegraph was started, to carry messages quickly from place to place ; but I think it was still more wonderful when men laid wires, or cables, under the sea, so that messages could be sent from England to all parts of the world. All these improvements were regarded with interest by the Queen, and it pleased her to see her people growing better and happier in this greater freedom of communication.

I must now tell you of an event which took place when she was twenty-one. You know a queen always chooses her own husband, and Queen Victoria chose to marry her young German cousin, Prince Albert of Saxe-Coburg and Gotha, nephew of Leopold, King of the Belgians. There were great rejoicings on the wedding-day (February 10, 1840), and the marriage proved a very happy one for the Queen and the country.

The birth of a son at the end of the following year was again the cause of much rejoicing in England. He was christened Albert Edward, and succeeded his mother on the throne of England fifty-nine years later, as King Edward the Seventh.

One of the Queen's first acts after this was to pay a visit to Louis Philippe, King of France, whose daughter had married her uncle, Leopold, King of the Belgians. It was the first time an English sovereign had set foot in France since Henry the Eighth had appeared on the Field of the Cloth of Gold.

Some years later, the people of France grew discontented with the weak government of Louis Philippe. Fighting often took place in the streets, until matters ended in a complete revolution. Louis Philippe, in terror for his life, made his escape from Paris and, disguised as a peasant, fled to England with his poor old wife. It has ever been England's pride, that she receives exiles in distress from other countries, and the Queen now placed the royal residence of Claremont, in Surrey, at the disposal of the French king and his dethroned queen.

This revolution in France led to revolutions in other countries. In England a number of discontented people, some of whom had been thrown out of work by the use of the new machinery, thought that a new charter, drawn up by them, would ensure better food and wages. They were called Chartists, and they thought the moment had come when they might frighten the Queen and Parliament into granting their requests. So they collected in huge numbers and decided to go in a procession to the House of Commons to present a petition signed by hundreds and thousands of people. Riots were feared, and the Queen, with her young children, was hurried out of London. But the people of England loved their Queen too well to let the Chartists gain the day. Under the old Duke of Wellington, soldiers were placed in various parts of London ; the principal citizens guarded the city, while policemen kept the bridges over the Thames. The Chartists had planned their great procession with the monster petition, for the tenth of April, but when that day came, and they found that the people of London were against them, they wisely dispersed and went quietly home.

So you see, while there had been fighting between the people and the soldiers of all the great cities of Europe about this time, there was, after all, peace in London on the memorable Tenth of April, 1848.

In Ireland, I am sorry to say, matters were not so peaceful

A very sad thing had happened early in the Queen's reign, which had greatly distressed her. A terrible famine had taken place in Ireland, caused by a disease, which destroyed the potato crop. The potato is the chief food of the poor people in Ireland, and when the potatoes rotted in the ground, there was nothing left for them to live upon. The rich people in England did all they could to help, and Parliament voted large sums of money, but thousands and thousands died of disease and starvation, until poor Ireland had lost two millions of her people. The country was still suffering from the effects of famine when rebellion broke out.

It distressed the Queen to think that she had disloyal subjects across the water, so when the country was quiet again, she and Prince Albert paid their first visit to Ireland, where they were received with great enthusiasm.

But, my dear Arthur, the discontent in Ireland was too deeply rooted to be so easily cured, and you will hear of more troubles there before the end of Queen Victoria's reign and indeed for years after that.

There had, for some time, been a cry in England for cheaper food, for all food coming into the country from abroad was heavily taxed. The Irish famine had shown how important it was not to depend too much on home crops alone. If the tax on foreign corn were removed, people in England could get cheaper bread ; but, on the other hand, the farmers would get a lower price for their home-grown corn. So there was a great outcry at this suggestion. But after a time, Sir Robert Peel managed to pass a Bill through the House of Commons doing away with the tax on corn. The result of this was that bread became much cheaper throughout the United Kingdom. Other taxes were gradually removed, and England had what is known as Free

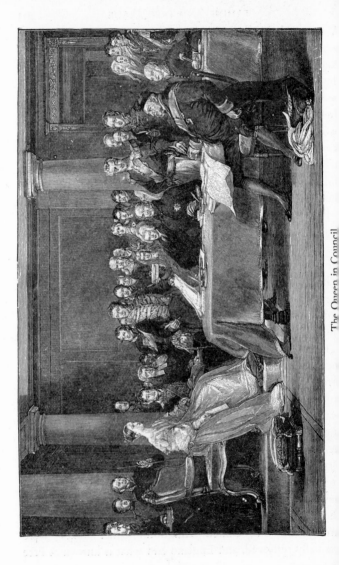

The Queen in Council

Trade, that is to say, she could import things from other countries without paying taxes on them. And so it remained for many years, much to the prosperity of the people, until for other causes it had to be altered, but of that I need not tell you now.

It was a sad day for England when the Duke of Wellington died, at the age of eighty-four. He was greatly missed by the Queen and the whole nation. He had been loved and trusted during the whole of his long life, and the people of London gave him a public funeral, such as had never been seen before. He was laid in St. Paul's Cathedral, beside the great sea-captain Nelson ; and you must never forget the names of these two great men, who did so much for their country. Their names are joined in the fine ode which Tennyson, the poet-laureate of the Queen's reign, wrote in memory of the Duke. I advise you, Arthur, to read this poem for yourself. It is called "An Ode on the Death of the Duke of Wellington."

England had cause to mourn the loss of the " Iron Duke," as he was called, a few years later, when the long peace of forty years was broken by war with Russia.

But you shall hear of this in the next chapter.

CHAPTER LXI

QUEEN VICTORIA—(*continued*)

Ever since the great battle of Waterloo, England had been at peace. And you can imagine how sad the Queen was when she heard that her beloved country must soon be at war. The Russians, whose land, you know, is the largest in Europe, were trying to get possession of Turkey. England feared, if Russia were successful, that she would grow too powerful in the East. So the English and French joined together to help the Turks to keep Russia in check.

Most of the fighting took place in the Crimea, a peninsula to the south of Russia, for it was here that Russia had established a great fortress and arsenal. The first battle, fought by the river Alma, ended in the defeat of the Russians. The next, at Balaclava, has been made famous by the charge of the Light Brigade. This brigade received an order to retake some guns captured by the Russians. Officers and men feared there was some mistake, but rather than disobey superior orders, they heroically made the charge. Six hundred of them rode bravely forward, to find themselves right under the Russian guns. Some one had blundered, and only two hundred returned from the fatal charge. The battle of Inkerman followed, with another Russian defeat. Still the fortress of Sebastopol defied the English and French armies. Winter came on. The sufferings of our soldiers were terrible. They had no proper shelter from the icy storms that swept over the Crimea, no warm clothes, and not enough food.

The Charge of the Heavy Brigade at Balaclava.

A band of Englishwomen, under Florence Nightingale, heroically undertook the long journey to the Crimea in order to nurse the poor soldiers in hospital.

At last, with the fall of Sebastopol, the unhappy war came to an end.

When the English soldiers came home, the Queen had a medal struck as a reward for bravery. It was made from the cannon taken at Sebastopol, and was in the shape of a cross, which was called the Victoria Cross. The Queen herself presented it to those who had been specially brave, thanking them for their courage and devotion. To win that Cross is the greatest honour possible to a soldier or a sailor.

The soldiers had not been home very long before a terrible mutiny broke out in India among the Sepoys. The Sepoys are Indians whom the English trained to be soldiers in the service of the East India Company, of which you have already heard. They were supposed to be faithful to their English masters, but they had been discontented for some time.

A belief had spread among them that the English were trying to destroy their religion and take away their old privileges. You know that cows are held sacred by many Indians. One day some new cartridges were given to the Indian soldiers, which were covered with the grease of cow's fat to keep out the wet. The soldiers had to bite these cartridges in their mouths before loading. When they heard of this, they regarded it as a deadly insult ; and as they were already discontented by the stories which had been spread among them, they determined to mutiny and kill their English masters. This they did, without pity or mercy, and general terror spread through the land.

At Cawnpore the English garrison was under an old man of seventy-five. Unable to get help, he accepted the assistance of a native, whom he trusted, called Nana Sahib. This man played him false. He offered to conduct the women and children, with their sick and wounded men, across the river Ganges to safety ; but they had no sooner reached the boats

An Officer of First Royal Regiment of Foot, 1838.

and pushed off from the land than, at a given signal, he had them fired upon and killed. Some few escaped, and these he had shut up in a place, where there was neither air nor light. After untold sufferings, they died. It is one of the saddest stories in English history, but it is relieved by the splendid heroism of the defence of Lucknow by Sir Henry Lawrence, and the assault of Delhi by John Nicholson.

When the mutiny broke out, Sir Henry Lawrence set to work to strengthen the garrison at Lucknow, where he was besieged by the natives. He had women and children to defend, for all were shut up in the Residency together. By day and night he worked at his post, until he was killed by a shell which burst in his room.

" Never give up, I charge you. Every man die at his post."

This was his dying command. Already the English flag, floating from the roof, was riddled with shot. Already men, women, and children, were growing weak from want of food, but those brave men defended the cluster of buildings occupied by the English, called " the Residency," to the last. And when Generals Havelock and Outram fought their way to the relief of Lucknow, the English there could cry with honest pride, that they had defended their Residency for nearly five months.

When peace was restored, it was decided to end the rule of the East India Company, and to put India under the government of the Queen and her Ministers. Later on, the Queen took the title of Empress of India. Her Indians became some of the most faithful subjects and devoted attendants at the English Court.

It is impossible to tell you everything that happened in this long reign, but I think you will like to hear how the idea of Volunteers arose at this time.

England and France were no longer the good friends they had been. Indeed, they had become so suspicious of one another, that it was feared in England that the French might one day invade her coasts. People became alarmed, thinking there were not soldiers enough to defend her shores. So men of every class came forward of their own free will, to be drilled and trained as soldiers in case of war. These Volunteers, as they were called, were formed into regiments. The French invasion did not take place, but ever since this time a volunteer force has formed part of the home defence, though now it is a real part of the Army, and its officers and men are called Territorials.

Now I am coming to one of the saddest events of this reign. The Queen had been married for twenty-one years, when her devoted husband, Prince Albert, died ; leaving her with nine children. The whole nation mourned with the widowed Queen, who was, for a time, crushed by the blow that had fallen upon her, and it was many years before she quite recovered from it ; but always she was helped by her sons and daughters, and especially by the young Prince of Wales, who was afterwards King Edward.

In the Queen's long reign, many new laws were made for the greater happiness and freedom of her people. You remember about the Reform Bill, which was passed in the reign of William IV., allowing all big towns to send one or two members to Parliament, according to the number of people in every town. Only a certain number of rich people were allowed to elect these members, and a feeling had long been growing among the working men of England, that they too ought to have a voice in the election of the man who was to represent them in Parliament. So another Reform Bill was drawn up. It allowed every working man to have a vote, if he paid a certain amount of rates and taxes, that is to say, if he bore his share of the expenses of the government. And so, from that time, the greater number of working men have had a voice in managing the affairs of the nation. Further than this, a Ballot Act was passed, making all voting secret ;

so that every man could vote for whom he liked, without any one else knowing whom he had supported. And since then further reforms have been made so that every man and every woman too, who is fairly entitled to it, has a vote.

The tax, too, was taken off paper. When Queen Victoria came to the throne, a daily newspaper cost sixpence, and could only be bought by rich people. It was common for a number of people to club together and take in a paper, which they read by turn. You can imagine how pleased these men were, when it was made possible for each one to buy his paper for one penny.

All these improvements were for the benefit of grown-up people ; but a great deal was done for the children of England, as you shall now hear. Perhaps the passing of the Education Act in 1870 was one of the most important events in the whole reign.

In the early part of the reign very few children could read or write. Indeed, worse than this, numbers of them were made to work underground in dark mines for fifteen hours a day. When the people of England realized this, they at once tried to put a stop to it. A good man, called Lord Shaftesbury, took up the cause of the children, and brought in a Bill to shorten their hours.

For some time past, schools had been established all over England in connection with the Churches. They were chiefly supported by presents of money from rich people, and were known as voluntary schools. Teachers were specially trained to teach the children, and a great deal of very good work was done. But the population of England had been rapidly increasing, and there were hundreds and thousands of little children who had no school to go to. I am sorry to tell you that England was behind other countries in the training of her children. France and Germany had already built schools, and compelled their children to attend.

At last England followed their example. Schools sprang up all over the country, under the management of chosen bodies of people in each place, known as School Boards, while the voluntary schools still continued with renewed energy ; so that soon, education was provided for every child in the country. Some years later, every child was compelled to attend school for a certain number of years, free of all expense.

I shall end this chapter by telling you of something that caused great rejoicing in England. The Queen's eldest son, Albert Edward, Prince of Wales, married the beautiful Princess Alexandra, daughter of the King of Denmark. The country gave the new Princess such a welcome, as must have gladdened the heart of the poor widowed Queen.

CHAPTER LXII

QUEEN VICTORIA—(*continued*)

I have now come to a very important part of Queen Victoria's reign—the enormous increase of her commerce, and the growth of her great Colonies. As you will very often hear these two subjects mentioned, I will try to explain them to you.

Once the power of steam had been discovered, there seemed no end to all its uses. Not only could it move engines drawing carriages along metal lines, not only could it move ships through the water, but it could turn machines, which, up to this time, had been turned by the hands of man. This meant greater speed, and increase of work. Some day you will see a great factory, and learn for yourself the wonderful things that a steam-engine and electricity can do ; how these forces are used to make cloth, linen, flannel, as well as knives and tools and many other things which are of daily use in every home.

The English were among the first people to discover the power of steam, and they went on inventing new machines to help their increasing work. It is not possible to tell you about one-half of these wonderful inventions here, but I want you to understand the great importance of these machines, and the great increase of commerce and wealth they brought to England. Take, for instance, the clothes you wear. There is cloth for your coat ; flannel, linen, or silk for your shirt ; wool for your stockings ; and leather for your boots. You are but one of the millions of little boys who wear these things, so that you can form an idea of what quantities are made. It is only by means of machinery working at great speed that this can be done ; and as the English were among the first to invent these machines, so, for many years, they made a great part of the clothing of the world. Other nations have now followed, but still she provides a great part.

But she cannot supply sheep enough for the wool, nor flax enough for the linen, and she cannot grow cotton at all. So that these had to be brought over from other countries in ships. As trade increased, so more and more ships were wanted to bring the raw material, as it is called, to England, and to take back ready-made goods to other countries.

Once there was a great civil war in America. The northern states fought against the southern states on the question of slavery. England had given up slavery long before this, so the question did not matter to her ; but most of her cotton came from the southern states. While the war lasted, no cotton could be grown to send to England. The cotton mills in Lancashire had to be closed ; thousands of people were thrown out of work and nearly starved. This will show you how one country depends on another for its prosperity and how evil war is, even hurting people very far away from the scene of the conflict.

But when all the mills in the north were busy, when people were well and prosperous, when trade was growing, and wealth increasing, then the people found they had been increasing too, and their numbers were too large for England to find work for them all. So a great many of them sailed away beyond the seas to make new homes. Some went to

10*

Canada, and sent over grain and farm produce to England ; some went to Australia to keep sheep, so that they could send wool to England, and others went to South Africa where there are mines of diamonds and gold.

This brings us to the growth of the British colonies, and you will like to hear how well Englishmen did, when they went to live far away from home.

You remember how we lost our American colonies in the reign of George the Third, but how, just before this, General Wolfe had won Quebec, the capital of Canada, from the French. Since those days Canada had grown. A great many English had made their homes there. Gradually they had made their way westward ; they had cut down trees, cleared the forests, dug up new soil, and planted crops. After a time, Canada stretched from sea to sea, right across from the Atlantic to the Pacific Ocean. It became known as the Dominion of Canada ; but the east and the far west were like two countries, until they were joined by means of a great railway, known as the Canadian-Pacific Railway.

This has made communication easy to all parts, and colonists can forward their grain to the home country without difficulty. They can also travel to Ottawa, where the central government sits, to arrange the affairs of the Dominion. For Canada is a " self-governing colony," that is to say, the English colonists are allowed to manage the affairs of their own country, though they are proud to feel they are still a loyal part of the British Empire and under the British sovereign.

All the northern part of the country is bitterly cold. It extends right up into the Arctic regions, where the sea is frozen for a great part of the year. For a long time, explorers had been sailing about these northern seas, trying to find a

North-West Passage from the Atlantic through the ice north of Canada to the Pacific Ocean. They hoped to find a short way for ships to sail to India from England, without going round by the Cape of Good Hope.

You will like to hear a little about Sir John Franklin, the man who really found the North-West Passage at last. He started off with two ships, and a hundred and thirty men. At first all went well, then there was silence. Year after year passed by, and there was no news of Franklin. Ship after ship went in search of him, but it was twelve years before it was discovered for certain that he and all his brave companions had died of cold and starvation.

But, although he had found the North-West Passage before he died, it was no use for ships sailing to India, because it was never altogether open and free from ice. Another way, however, was soon after this opened to India. For a clever Frenchman cut through a piece of land between the Mediterranean and the Red Sea, making the Suez Canal, by which all ships can sail to India, without going round by the Cape of Good Hope.

Besides Canada, another British country sprang up, though it was much farther away from England, across the seas—I mean Australia. This great country, far beyond India, had been discovered by Captain Cook in the reign of George III. At first it seemed so far away, that only convicts were sent there from the English prisons. But early in the reign, other English people went out ; and when gold was discovered there in 1851, there was quite a rush of colonists. Two new colonies sprang up, and in the course of time they were called Victoria and Queensland, which shows you that Englishmen never forget their home, however far away they may be. Since those days, Australia has grown very rapidly. It is largely a sheep-farming colony, and meat is sent frozen all the way home for us to eat.

Australia has its own Parliament, with representatives from each of its states, just as Canada has ; and the British in both countries like to feel that they are still a part of their beloved homeland. They could separate if they liked, to become independent nations like France and Germany, but I am glad to say that our colonies are not like that. They would rather be parts of our great British Empire, and are ready, in case of danger, to take their places by our side, as we should be with them if they were threatened.

Near Australia lies the sister colony of New Zealand. The first colonists arrived here two years after the Queen's accession, and they called their capital Wellington, after the Duke.

Our possessions also grew in Africa. Immense tracts of land there came under British protection during the reign of Queen Victoria.

In the reign of George the Third, the Cape of Good Hope became English. It was taken from the Dutch, but I am sorry to say the English and Dutch who had to live together at the Cape did not agree very well. Just about the time when the Queen began to reign, the Dutch farmers—or Boers, as they were called—refused to live under the British rule any longer ; and went off to live by themselves farther north, in a little-known part of Africa. They went beyond the Vaal river, so their country was called the Transvaal.

The English also had trouble with the natives, as well as with the Boers. There was a very powerful tribe of black men called Zulus, who wanted to drive out the British, and there was some terrible fighting, though the British conquered at last. A very sad thing happened in one of these

Zulu wars. Prince Louis Napoleon, whose father—once Emperor of France—had died an exile in England, was killed while fighting on the side of the British, to the great grief of the Queen.

Besides the colonists in Africa, there were explorers and travellers. One of these was David Livingstone. He opened up Central Africa, and discovered some of the great lakes. He was a missionary, and taught the heathen about Christ, and the black people loved him. So that, when he died far away from home, in the very heart of Africa, two black servants carried his body all the way to the coast, across hundreds of miles, to be buried by his white friends at Zanzibar.

A great discovery of diamonds caused a rush of colonists to South Africa. One Englishman named Cecil Rhodes made a great fortune in the diamond mines. He spent his money in the country, and helped England to gain an immense tract of land to the north of Natal, which was called after him, Rhodesia.

Up to this time, the Boers had lived in the Transvaal apart from the English, as I told you. But a great discovery of gold in their country brought a number of English colonists there. This displeased them, and they refused to let the English take any part in the government, so after a time war broke out. At first the Boers were successful, and our troops were shut up in Ladysmith and Mafeking for many months. At length larger armies were sent out from England under Lord Roberts, and the Boers were gradually forced back into their own country. This war was still going on when Queen Victoria died. But very soon afterwards peace was made, and so wise an arrangement was reached with the Boers that after a time they became contented citizens of the Empire, and in the Great War, of which I must tell you presently, fought for South Africa against the Germans and under two of their old Boer generals, Botha and Smuts, gained a victory of which we all are proud.

On the Gold Coast of West Africa, England has possessions too, though this was a very unhealthy part for white men to live in. The English had a good deal of fighting with the black King of Ashanti, before he would allow them to enter his country; but he was such a tyrannical ruler that our Government felt it must interfere. Soon after this, another large tract of country, known as Nigeria, was placed under the protection of England, for here, too, the people were oppressed. And you know, my dear Arthur, wherever there is English rule, there is freedom and justice.

When I have mentioned Uganda, I think I shall have told you about all our largest possessions in Africa. So you see how our country has stretched out her arms far and wide—to America, to Australia, and to Africa, and how she has sons and daughters living in these great continents. They are loyal to her, and ready to help her in times of peril and danger, while she is ever ready to protect them.

So whereas in the beginning of the great Queen's reign, England had only the little colony of Canada; at the end, she had many large colonies, now called Dominions, of the utmost importance. Her foreign possessions had grown to be ninety times the size of herself, and three times the size of all Europe put together. The Queen no longer ruled over the British Isles only, as the Kings and Queens of England had done before her, but over a great Empire beyond the seas as well; so that when her son came to the throne, he was called not only King of England, but also King of the British Dominions over the sea.

An Old Wooden Battleship.

CHAPTER LXIII

QUEEN VICTORIA—(*continued*)

I have told you how England has taken whole countries under her care to administer justice to oppressed people, and I now want to tell you a little about Burma and Egypt. They are not Dominions like Canada, Australia, and parts of Africa, where white men go to make their homes. They are countries full of their own people, and Englishmen help them to rule their country more justly than before, as they have done in India.

In the case of Burma, or Farther India, as it used to be called, our rulers found that King Theebaw was ill-treating our traders who visited his country, so we deposed him and assumed control of it ourselves. It is now a part of the British Empire.

But it was quite different in Egypt. This country was governed by a native ruler, called the Khedive, who was England's friend. Another native, called Arabi, resented this English friendship, and revolted. English troops were sent, and Arabi was defeated and taken prisoner.

More fighting took place after this, because an Arab chief, calling himself the "Mahdi," invaded the country farther up the Nile. He had a number of followers who believed in him, and they destroyed an English army, that was sent from Cairo against them. Then a gallant soldier, General Gordon, who knew Egypt well, was sent out from England. He rode through the desert on a camel to Khartoum, where

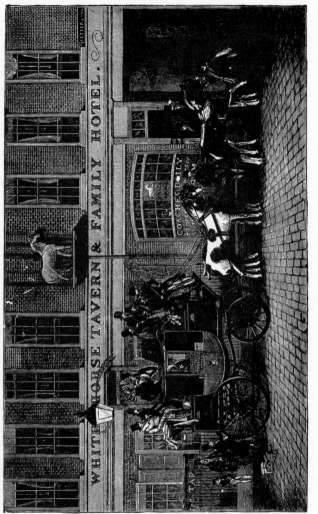

An Old Stage Coach.

he was besieged for a long time by the Mahdi's troops. At last British soldiers were sent to his relief; but I am sorry to say they arrived too late, for General Gordon was killed the very day they appeared at Khartoum.

Some years after this, General Kitchener, with brave English and Egyptian soldiers, fought and won back the Sudan. This immense tract of country watered by the Nile is now Anglo-Egyptian, which means that both the British and the government of the Khedive are responsible for its good government.

You will like to hear how things were getting on at home all this time. Lord Beaconsfield, one of the Queen's favourite ministers, had died, and Mr. Gladstone had succeeded him. This change gave a great chance to the Irish. A number of them wished to have a separate Parliament to sit in Dublin, as it did in the old days. They had a clever leader in Mr. Parnell, and they persuaded Mr. Gladstone to bring in a Bill to give them Home Rule—that is, the power to govern themselves and make their own laws. For some years the people of England and Ireland were greatly agitated over this; but a general election decided that the Irish should not have a Parliament of their own, but that they should continue to sit at Westminster with the Scottish and Welsh members.

The Queen had a beautiful house in Scotland called Balmoral, where she spent some months every year. She was eighty-one when she went over to Ireland, which country she had not visited for forty years. It must have been a great effort, but she was very pleased with the hearty welcome she received from the warm-hearted Irish.

It is pleasant to turn to the celebration of the Queen's first Jubilee. She had reigned over England for fifty years, a period only exceeded by Edward the Third and George the

Third. A special thanksgiving service was held at Westminster Abbey to celebrate the event. In front of the long procession rode thirty-two princes of her own house, including her sons, her grandsons, and her sons-in-law, and the Crown Prince of Prussia, Frederick, who was married to our Queen's eldest daughter, and who died in the next year, just after he had become German Emperor.

But I must tell you something of the Diamond Jubilee. In the year 1897 the Queen had reigned for sixty years, which was longer than any English ruler had reigned before. If the first Jubilee procession had been splendid, this one was yet more splendid. Such a royal progress had never passed through London before, for there were subjects there from every part of the great Empire. They had all come across the sea to do honour to the Queen under whose rule they were living so happily. The procession made its way to St. Paul's Cathedral amid a roar of applause, for the Queen had won all hearts by her kind deeds and motherly ways. People sang " God save the Queen " as she passed, and at night the whole country was illuminated.

But perhaps the most important part of this famous Jubilee was the great naval review that took place at Spithead. Amid the ships of other nations in their long imposing lines, the strength of the British navy showed forth in its pride and glory. All through the reign of Queen Victoria, the navy had been growing steadily and surely ; and this was very necessary, for England has a smaller standing army than any other nation. Since the days of Nelson, she has had command of the sea, she must therefore look to her fleet as her chief protection and her " all-in-all."

Now London was a very different place from what it had been sixty years before. Better houses had been built for rich and poor ; the streets were cleaned, and lit with electric light and gas ; policemen kept the crowds in better order while the people themselves were better fed and dressed. Then the new Houses of Parliament had been built at Westminster, the new Tower Bridge had been made over the Thames, new Law Courts had arisen, and many of the narrow streets had been made broader.

You would like to hear something about Queen Victoria's family, I am sure, before I end this chapter. Her eldest daughter became the wife of the Emperor Frederick of Germany, and mother of the Emperor (or Kaiser) against whom we fought the terrible war of 1914. Her eldest son, who afterwards was King Edward the Seventh, married a Danish princess, and she became Queen Alexandra. They had two sons and three daughters of whom the second son was our beloved King George the Fifth, whose eldest-born is our present gracious Sovereign.

I am sorry to say the last years of Queen Victoria's life were clouded by the war in South Africa. She lived long enough to receive Lord Roberts on his return home, but her strength was failing rapidly, and she died on January 22, 1901, at the age of eighty-one. She had lived longer than her grandfather, George III., by just a few days. Her people wished her to be buried in Westminster Abbey, but she had long before decided to be laid beside her husband at Windsor. So they gave her a splendid funeral, and buried her in the grave that she had chosen. And they praised her stainless life and her devotion to duty ; for not only Great Britain and the Empire, but the whole world, had lost one of its best friends.

CHAPTER LXIV

EDWARD VII.—1901 TO 1910

Queen Victoria had been so loved by her people, and her death had caused such sorrow all over the world, that it seemed as if King Edward the Seventh would not have an easy task to follow her. Yet it is not too much to say that during his short reign of a little more than nine years, he became a more popular ruler than she had ever been.

As I have already told you, Queen Victoria had led a very quiet and retired life after the death of the Prince Consort. She was seldom seen in public, and if it had not been that her portrait was to be found in nearly every home in the land, few of her subjects would have known what she was like. But King Edward was known everywhere. As Prince of Wales he had for years taken his mother's place in performing public duties ; he was also a leader of London Society, a patron of sport of every description, and a country gentleman of the good old-fashioned kind. Wherever there was a ceremony of national importance, such as the opening of a university, a hospital, or a public library, he was there ; his horses had twice won the Derby, the most famous race in the world ; his sailing yachts had distinguished themselves at continental regattas ; and his estate at Sandringham was one of the best managed in England. Little wonder, then, that the people looked forward with joy to his reign : such a King could not fail to be popular.

And he was truly popular ; not at home only, but abroad

also. Owing to the large number of his relations who were kings and queens on the continent, he was sometimes called " the uncle of Europe " ; and there is no doubt that his welcome visits to foreign countries caused the name of England to be admired and respected in a way it had never been before. Wherever he went he left a feeling of friendship behind him, and if he is known among future generations by the title of " the Peacemaker " (as he was called by some of his admirers even before he died), he will have won more lasting fame than many of the noblest warrior monarchs of the past.

When he came to the throne the Boer war was still dragging on, but both sides were tired of it. King Edward from the first used his influence to bring it to an end, so that his coronation might be celebrated in peace. So the Boer generals met ours at a little place called Vereeniging, and the result of the conference was that the Boers had to admit that they were beaten and to lay down their arms. They had fought bravely and fairly, and, as we are never hard on people we have conquered, they were treated kindly, and as we have seen since, wisely. Though it is a bitter thing for a free people to be deprived of their independence, there is little doubt that they were better off in the end, for they now enjoy freedom as equal members with the British settlers in the Union of South Africa and a security they never had before.

Many years had passed, as you know, since the English had seen a King crowned, so all the nation was looking forward with pleasure to the day when King Edward would pass through the streets of London, in all his majesty, to Westminster Abbey. Wonderful preparations were made, and everything was ready ; but almost at the last minute word was passed round that he was seriously ill, and the ceremony had to be postponed. He was not a young man, and the large amount of extra work he had tried to do had proved too much for him. Luckily a clever surgeon performed an operation in time, and his life was saved ; he gradually recovered, and when his coronation really did take place, three months later, the greatest joy and thankfulness were felt through the length and breadth of the land.

Towards the end of the same year Prince George, who had been created Duke of Cornwall on the death of Queen Victoria, was made Prince of Wales—a title which his father had borne with such honour for nearly sixty years. Soon after this he went with his Princess, in a fine ship called the *Ophir*, on a round of visits to the British countries beyond the seas. His most important journey was to Australia, where the different states had decided to join together into one " Commonwealth." The Prince went to give the King's greeting to the new government and to wish it success ; and so well has it prospered since then that it is now able to send battleships and men to help our navy and army.

You may be sure that on his travels our Prince saw much to be proud of ; but he also saw some things that were not so satisfactory. When he returned home he told what he had seen to the leading merchants of London, warned them of the progress that other nations were making in the distant corners of the earth, and advised old England to "wake up " and look after its trade. For he saw how important to our Empire our trade is : and that all its parts should do what they can to work with and help the other parts, in a great inspiring brotherhood.

Now I think I ought to tell you how King Edward's accession was celebrated in India. Nearly twenty-five years before this, Queen Victoria had been proclaimed Empress of

India, so it was decided that it would be a good thing to have a gathering of the native princes to do homage to their new sovereign. A big assembly, called a Durbar, was held at Delhi, the old capital of the Mogul rulers, and all the Indian chiefs and kings were summoned to it. As the King could not be present himself, his Viceroy took his place, and the princes came before him one by one and took the oath of loyalty to their Emperor. This was a very wise precaution to take, since the Indians who remembered the bad days of the Mutiny would be less likely to rebel again when they knew that their rulers had agreed to serve the English King. Since then our government in England has tried to make the various races of India take a greater interest in their own affairs, and has built a great system of government, so that in time to come they may be allowed to manage their own country themselves.

One of the earliest and most important events in King Edward's reign was the formation of an alliance with Japan. Perhaps I ought to go back a little, to tell you what had been happening in what is called " the Far East." China, in spite of its great superiority in numbers, had been badly defeated in war a few years before by little Japan, and had lost some of its most important towns as well as the large island of Formosa. Russia was jealous of Japan's success, and said she would be too powerful if she kept all she had taken from China, so (in order to make things more even) she stepped in and took some of them for herself, especially the wonderful fortress of Port Arthur in the Korea. This led to trouble, as the Japanese just waited for an opportunity to attack Russia, and to win back the places she had taken. War soon broke out. The fighting on land was terrible ; no such slaughter had been heard of before then. On sea also, where the

Japanese were the more powerful, there was very severe fighting, but in the end the Russian ships were nearly all captured or sunk, so they thought they had better end the war. Peace was arranged, on condition that Russia gave back to Japan most of the places which she had taken from her. The Japanese were glad to make closer friendship with a strong European power, and so our alliance with them was made and maintained for a number of years.

You have already been told that King Edward made friends wherever he went. No sooner had he ascended the throne than he began his travels. Lisbon, Rome, and Paris were visited in turn, while Scotland and Ireland were not neglected. You know that Queen Victoria had been very fond of Scotland and its people, who were also very fond of her ; but Ireland had been very bitter towards England for a long time. This feeling King Edward set himself to remove ; and it is certain that his friendly and open manner quite charmed the hearts of the Irish people. But unhappily other influences spoilt the good work and poor Ireland is still torn by angers and distrust.

Of all foreign countries France was certainly his favourite. As Prince of Wales he had been popular with the French people, and they were glad to find that when he became King his affection for their nation increased rather than diminished. In his official meetings with their President Loubet, and afterwards with President Fallières, they were quick to notice an element of personal friendliness and courtesy, and the interchange of visits by the two fleets which followed, set them talking about an *entente cordiale* with England. This expression, which means rather more than " a good understanding " and rather less than " a treaty," will help you to understand King Edward's wonderful power of attracting alliances.

This *rapprochement*—" drawing nearer "—of France was,

you may be sure, not altogether pleasing to Germany, who was always saying she was afraid of being hemmed in on all sides by enemies, and was anxious not to have England against her. It is true that, if she had really meant to keep on good terms with us, she might have acted more wisely than she did. She had built a big navy, on the excuse that it was needed to protect her commerce, and had dug an immense canal from the Baltic to the North Sea, through which the largest ships could pass without difficulty. She had also fortified the island of Heligoland, which we had rather unwisely given to her some years before, in exchange for some small places in Africa ; and the English people were beginning to wonder what all these warlike preparations meant. Still, the German Emperor continued to appear friendly towards our people, and his visits to England and the reception of our King and Queen in Berlin seemed to foretell that the feeling of jealousy might disappear, and a new era of trust and confidence arise between the two nations. But, as you will hear later, that was not to be, because those in Prussia who wished to have a war could not be controlled ; and all the time they were getting ready and secretly plotting for it to break out. Our great soldier, Lord Roberts, who knew something of what was going on in Prussia, did his best to arouse the British people to the dangers threatened by a powerful Germany ; but they did not really listen to him, and when war did afterwards break out our country was not sufficiently prepared for it.

And now let us see what had been happening at home. The Conservative party had been in power for a long time, and it was evident that the country wanted a change. When the election at last took place the Liberals had such a huge majority that they believed the people wished them to make great changes in the laws, so they proceeded to do so. The first thing they did was to create a new army system, to enable our forces to be rapidly increased during war. This was a good thing (though many thought it did not go far enough), and nobody really objected to it ; but when they wished to give Home Rule to Ireland and also attacked the privileges of the landowners they came into conflict with the House of Lords, which has always been Conservative in its sympathies. At this time a new party began to appear in Parliament. It consisted generally of workmen who thought that as they had votes they might well use those votes for themselves, and so the Labour Party began to compete for government against the Liberals and the Conservatives.

The quarrel between the two Houses of Parliament went on for some years. More than once the Lords gave way, but at length they brought matters to a head by refusing to pass the Budget for the year. As the Budget provides the money for carrying on the government, it is clear that if no money is voted the government cannot go on. So they were obliged to have an election to find out on whose side the country was ; and as the verdict was against the Lords they had to accept the Budget. After this the Liberals wanted to prevent such a thing happening again, and brought in a Bill to limit the power of the Upper House. Party feeling ran very high, and just as it seemed to have reached its bitterest point the newspapers announced that King Edward had been taken suddenly ill ; and almost before the people had time to realize that his ailment was serious he was dead.

The news of this sad event, which occurred on May 6th, 1910, came as a shock not only to the Empire, but to the whole world, and the British nation was touched by the expressions of sympathy which came from all sides. No such

collection of kings and princes had ever been seen as followed
in his funeral procession. The German Emperor came in
person and rode alongside of our new King George the Fifth ;
while the French mourned the lost " Edouard " as if he had
been one of their own flesh and blood.

And now it is time to glance at what King Edward did for
his Oversea Dominions, for you must not forget that although
he had such wonderful success with foreigners his first care
was for his own subjects. At the beginning of his reign he
had sent the Prince of Wales to Australia, South Africa, and
Canada ; but a more famous journey still was the tour that
he made through India a few years later : so when King
George succeeded his father, it was said that he was the first
British Sovereign who had visited all his dominions. These
visits have drawn the Britons over the sea closer to the
Motherland, and this sympathy has been helped by Imperial
conferences in London, to which the Dominion and Colonial
Premiers now come as a matter of equality and right.

Not only in Australia, but also in South Africa, things had
been moving towards a closer union. It may seem strange to
foreigners that we should be so ready to trust those who have
recently been fighting against us ; but it has always been our
way, and this is one of the reasons why England has proved
herself so good a mother of colonies. She once lost a mighty
Empire—the present United States—by treating the people
carelessly ; she is not likely to make the same mistake again.
Well, soon after the Boer war was over our Government
made up their minds to let the new dominions manage their
own affairs ; and not many years later the English provinces
decided to join them, and to make one single State. The very
man who had led the Boer armies against us, General Botha,
was the first Premier of United South Africa. Even before

this memorable event took place, the conquered Transvaal had given a proof of its loyalty by sending to our King and Queen the Cullinan diamond, the biggest gem of its kind in the world, to take an honoured place among the crown jewels.

King Edward's reign, though short, was a time of many changes. One of the most remarkable movements was the demand of women for votes. Now I should like you to understand that a great many wise people were in favour of this ; but the question grew angry and embittered, and unhappily there was a good deal of violence before the reform was granted, as it was soon after the Great War began.

We have seen that the army was reorganized ; the same is true also of the navy. All of a sudden England surprised the world by building secretly a new kind of battleship, called the Dreadnought. This was so great an improvement on the vessels which had been built before, that all the nations in Europe set to work to imitate it, and so keen was the rivalry that even this wonderful ship soon got out of date. Another remarkable invention was the submarine, a boat which can travel for far distances either above or below the water. The French first built these, but, as usual, others copied them, and now every maritime nation has a fleet of these deadly craft.

The marvellous little engine which made the submarine possible was responsible for other developments also. Not only did it produce the motor-car, which is so common a sight in our streets to-day, but it also led to the building of the wonder of the age—flying machines. These were of two types : our English manufacturers paid especial attention to aeroplanes, while Germany made experiments chiefly with balloons driven by machinery.

And then, look at the progress of electricity. Its use for

" traction," or hauling vehicles, made an extraordinary difference to our lives. The street tram, the " tube " or underground railway, and the suburban electric trains soon became objects familiar to all dwellers in towns ; and people began to say it would not be long before horses and loco-motive engines would be superseded.

And, lastly, we must not forget to mention the marvellous discovery, by a clever Italian called Marconi, of wireless telegraphy. Since he found out a way of sending messages without wires it became possible to " talk " to ships far out at sea, and you will hardly need to be told what a great advantage that is, especially as through the " Wireless " you are familiar with its workings in your own home.

These are a few, but by no means all, of the blessings that King Edward's peaceful reign brought to the nation under his care.

CHAPTER LXV

GEORGE V.—1910 TO 1936

When George the Fifth came to the throne the people hoped that the good work done by his father would result in a long reign of peace ; but I am sorry to say that they were disappointed. Within the space of five years the Great Powers of Europe, as they were called, were locked together in the deadliest struggle that the world has ever seen, and England was brought nearer to ruin than ever she has been in her history. What it all arose from you will read later on ; but I think one of the chief reasons was that the nations had been so busy arming that a fight was bound to come sooner or later ; and Prussia especially wished to win a stronger position in the world through the use of her powerful army and her new navy.

But before I tell you of the Great War I want you to know how things had been going on at home. You will remember that just before King Edward died the Commons had been quarrelling with the Lords about which House was to have the chief power, and in the end the country decided that if they could not agree the Commons, or Lower House, was to have the last word. This was a great change, for the Lords had always before been allowed to say " No " when any laws were proposed that they did not think good for the country and some people think they ought to have this power still.

A gradual change had been coming over the House of Commons. As I told you, many working men had been elected members of Parliament, and their number increased at every election, so you will not be surprised to learn that more laws were passed to help the poorer classes. Old age pensions had already been granted to men and women who had reached the age of seventy and had not been able to save enough money to keep them when they were past working : this is a great and good Act, for it brings comfort and security to these poor people just when they need it most. In 1912 another Act was passed to help workers when they are ill, or out of work through no fault of their own. A workman pays so much a week, his employer also pays something, and the nation pays something more, so that when he is unable to earn wages he receives an allowance of money, and when he is ill a doctor has to attend him.

Ireland, you will remember, had for a long time been wishing to manage her own affairs, and at last seemed on the point of getting what she wanted. A Home Rule Bill had actually passed both Houses of Parliament, and was only waiting to be put into force when the Great War broke out. It was not thought wise to try the experiment when England was desperately at war, so the long-expected grant of Home Rule was postponed. I am afraid that this delay was one of the causes of the terrible revolution and fighting that took place in Ireland in the next few years.

And now we come to the tragedy that cast a gloom over every home for four long years and more and to which I have just referred—the Great World War. How and where did it begin ? I will tell you. In the Balkan peninsula, that part of Eastern Europe where many Christian races had long been under the government of the Turks, there were several little nations which had recently won their freedom. Russia had helped them to gain their independence, and considered

11

herself their protector ; but on the other side lay Austria, very jealous of this great power, and continually making trouble. As these little States were always quarrelling with one another, there had been many wars, and it needed very little to start another ; it was just as if a train of powder was waiting to have a match applied to it.

The heir to the Austrian throne and his wife were murdered while visiting a little place in Bosnia. Austria laid the blame of this senseless crime on Serbia, and demanded satisfaction and an apology. Though the Serbians denied that they were responsible, they agreed to do anything they could to appease Austria ; but the conditions that she made seemed so hard that they appealed to Russia for help. Now Russia was allied to France, and Austria was backed up by Germany, so you see that if war broke out it was certain that all these four nations would be drawn into it. So England did all she could to prevent an outbreak, reasoning with each power in turn. I think Austria might have given way, but Germany told her that she had gone too far to draw back, and in spite of all our efforts the war began. At first England did not join in, though she was suspicious of Germany and very friendly to France. But she only hesitated for four days, for the Germans suddenly invaded Luxemburg and Belgium, which had nothing whatever to do with the quarrel, in order to strike France in the back, so to speak : and this aroused the British nation. Many years before, the Great Powers had all agreed to protect Belgium from this very thing : even Germany had promised. When she was reminded of this, her Chancellor sneered at the treaty she had signed as " a scrap of paper " ; but England said the promise must be kept, or we should declare war. To this Germany returned no answer, so at eleven o'clock on August 4, 1914, when the limit of time expired, vast crowds of people assembled outside Buckingham Palace, and cheered King George to the echo, for standing up for poor down-trodden Belgium. They little thought that four long years of agony and distress would pass before they could cheer for the end of the fighting.

But one man foresaw it—Lord Kitchener. While nearly everybody was saying the war would not last till Christmas, and the German Kaiser was promising his troops that they would be home again " before the leaves fell," Lord Kitchener was asking men to enlist " for three years or the duration of the war."

Now I think I ought to explain that this war was like no war that had ever occurred before. In days gone by it was only the regular armies that fought ; and though the continental nations had for many years made all their men go through military training, we had kept only a small force, sufficient to prevent invasion and to guard our dominions across the seas : we had never thought we should have to join in a continental war. But now that we were mixed up in one we had to enlist every man that could serve, and no less than four million men volunteered. Even that was not enough, so in the end a law was passed that every sound man up to the age of fifty was obliged to defend his country, and for the first time in our history " conscription " became the law of the land. Not only did the men give their services, but the women also : they stepped into the places of those who had gone to the front, and " carried on " with their work. As time went on they joined various corps and wore uniforms, and hundreds of thousands of them risked their lives right in the middle of the war areas on the continent. No wonder the King and all Englishmen were proud of them, and thankful for their help !

I know you will be pleased to hear that when the mother country declared war all her dominions rushed to her aid. India, Canada, Australia, New Zealand—even South Africa, which had been fighting against us little more than ten years before—all sent soldiers and sailors to help us : no dependency was so small that it did not assist in some way, and nothing in our history has shown so clearly how wisely and kindly our colonies have been ruled in the past. Germany expected the British Empire to break up, but instead of that the war united it more closely than ever. Only in one place was there trouble—Ireland. A revolution broke out there in the south, but it was put down. Nevertheless, we had to keep a big army in Ireland all through the war, for fear the people might rise against us.

But it is time to talk of the fighting in Europe and elsewhere, though it is impossible to tell more than the smallest fraction of what happened. Before long, Italy, Portugal, and Roumania joined our side : Japan had done so at once, as she was our ally : Greece pretended to help us, but did not. America hesitated a long time, but the sinking of the *Lusitania* in 1917 by a German submarine, with the loss of over 1000 lives (many of them women and children), at last turned the scale, and she came in when help was badly needed.

On the other side Turkey joined Germany, and Bulgaria as well, not so much because she liked Germany as because she hated Serbia. So in Palestine, Mesopotamia, Italy, and all along the Eastern and Western fronts, the fighting went on day after day for more than four years. Millions of men were killed, and still more were injured for life. At the beginning the Germans nearly succeeded in capturing Paris. The gallant little British force sent out at once was forced to retreat almost as soon as it had taken up its position at Mons ;

Central Press

The Modern Army.
Fixing a gas mask.

but it rallied magnificently, and helped the French to win a
wonderful victory at the Marne river.   This victory, though
we did not know it at the time, decided the war, because
never again did the Germans come so near to success.

So fierce was the fighting that almost at the onset nearly
all our regular army was killed or wounded, so we had to
make haste to collect another ; and this took time.   But
when we had got the men we found we had not nearly
enough guns and ammunition, so the factories in England
were asked to leave what they were doing and make them ;
and men and women worked at it night and day.   By slow
degrees we got as many guns as the Germans had, but just
as things were beginning to look better a revolution broke
out in Russia.   The leaders of this revolution murdered the
unhappy Tsar and all his family, and said they would fight
no more ; so the Germans were now free to send all their
soldiers against the French and ourselves.   For a long time
we were in very great danger, but at last the American troops
began to arrive, and the tide turned.   Sir Douglas Haig drove
back a determined attack on Amiens, and the French Marshal
Foch, who had now been made Commander-in-Chief of all
the armies against Germany in France, ordered the whole
allied line to push forward.   Back, back went the Germans,
fighting desperately every inch of the way ; but they knew,
and all the world knew, that they were beaten.   At last their
armies got into such a tangle and were so demoralized that
they were forced to ask for an armistice.   It was granted,
and the war was over.   What a relief this armistice was,
only those who had fathers, sons or brothers in the fighting
line can really know.   The whole nation, the whole Empire,
was filled with gratitude and great relief.

But what had the Navy been doing ?   As King George had

London News Agency

H.M.S. "Hood."

foretold, it proved to be " Britain's sure shield." So well did it guard our shores that not a single soldier lost his life in crossing to or from the war from England or America. It fought only one really big battle, in the North Sea, off the coast of Jutland. Both sides lost many ships, but the victory was ours ; for although the German fleet luckily escaped home in the darkness, it never again dared to come out until it surrendered at the end of the war. As brave as the Navy, our Merchant Service also did splendid work. Though the seas all round our coasts were full of submarines, not one crew ever refused to leave port. This was a great blessing, for if our sailors had failed to bring us food we should have been forced by starvation to lose the war. As it was, our people passed through a very anxious time, and all food and coal had to be " rationed " : this meant that each person was given so much, and no more, so that supplies should not run out.

Not only was the war fought on sea and land, but in the air also. Airships and aeroplanes were everywhere, and a new terror was brought to the dwellers in our towns by attacks with bombs. London especially suffered from these, and a long time passed before we succeeded in checking those terrible raids.

I am sorry to say that hundreds were killed in this way who were not combatants in the war. Many women and children lost their lives through those bombing raids, and the people grew angry about it. But the Germans did many things that had never been done in war before : they used poison gas, they sank harmless merchantmen, and even torpedoed hospital ships. I am afraid that if ever we have another war more dreadful things still will happen, so it is to be hoped that everybody will try to make it impossible in the future.

It was with this object that the United States President, Woodrow Wilson, started the League of Nations ; but a majority of the American people refused to support him, and until they do support it, with all the other countries of the world, it cannot be as successful in preventing war as those must desire whose gospel is " Peace on Earth."

The state of Europe after the war was terrible. A vast area in France and Belgium was devastated ; whole towns were wiped out, and the nations who had taken part in the war were all so badly in debt that trade was brought almost to a standstill. For a while England prospered, but soon business began to fall away, and many thousands were unable to find work : at one time over two million men and women were out of employment.

In Germany the ruling sovereigns, it is true, were driven out, and republics were set up in the various states, but their commerce at first seemed all right, for when money was scarce the Germans used paper notes instead ; and for a while this plan succeeded. Before long this paper was found to be worth nothing, and those who had saved money were reduced to beggary. Notes for a million marks—a mark used to be equal to our shilling—were to be bought in London streets for a penny ; and they were not worth even that, being only scraps of paper. But now trade in Germany is again flourishing, and the country is so strongly organized and re-armed that the future is less settled than it has seemed since 1918.

Now it is time to see what changes have come in our own country. The most important, perhaps, is that women, in recognition of their fine work during the war, are now by law equal with men. They have votes : some are members of Parliament, and one has been in the Cabinet. They are

also taking their places in the learned professions. The Labour Party, too, has made great progress, and we have seen Labour Governments in charge of the affairs of the Kingdom. The south of Ireland, too, after centuries of rebellion and horrible civil war, has been made a free self-governing Dominion, like Canada ; but the northern province of Ulster still remains happily part of the United Kingdom, and, although it has its own Parliament, it also sends representatives to the Imperial Parliament at Westminster.

In our daily life there have been many changes : the most remarkable of these is wireless telephony, which allows us at our own fireside to listen to what is said or what is going on hundreds of miles away. We had looked forward to air travel becoming as common as the railway, but this has yet to come ; though more and more lines of aeroplanes are running regularly and carrying mails over Europe to India and between many countries.

But wonderful things have been done in the air since the war. A young American, named Lindbergh, flew from New York to Paris in May, 1927, a journey of 3,510 miles, in $33\frac{1}{4}$ hours ; and since then others have flown across the Atlantic and so far as from England to Australia in less than five days. In April, 1937, two Japanese flew their aeroplane, "Divine Wind," from Tokyo to Croydon, a distance of about 10,000 miles, in 94 hours.

In May, 1925, King George and Queen Mary opened an exhibition at Wembley, near London, in which every part of the British Empire showed what it could produce. In the autumn there was a meeting of statesmen of various countries at Locarno, and an agreement was made there, which was afterwards signed in London on the first of December. As a result of the Locarno Pact, as it is called, Germany entered the League of Nations, and in this way was helping to realize President Wilson's dream ; until, unfortunately, owing to its imperfect working, she left it again, as did Japan. But we hope that some day those great nations will rejoin the League, and the United States of America as well, for the cruel war that broke out in 1935 between Italy and Abyssinia, and, through a superiority of war machines but not of human courage, wiped out the ancient and independent Empire of Ethiopia, has shown how necessary such a union of the nations might be, especially to the weaker states.

I think that the most remarkable result of all, however, is the growth of respect and love felt for our Royal Family. Sorrow was shown by everybody when Queen Alexandra, the mother of the King, died on the 20th November, 1925. On the 21st April, 1926, a daughter was born to the Duchess and Duke of York, and this little girl, the Princess Elizabeth, with her sister, the Princess Margaret Rose, who was born on the 21st August, 1930, are in very truth the darlings of the nation.

At the end of 1928 the whole world waited anxiously for news of King George, who was very ill in Buckingham Palace. His illness was long, and it was not until the beginning of July, 1929, that His Majesty was strong enough to appear publicly and to attend a Thanksgiving Service for his recovery.

In the following years there was much anxiety in our country and throughout the world, for the prosperity which had been so great suddenly fell away and widespread depression in industry followed, with millions out of work and hardship everywhere.

Happily, our statesmen saw the necessity at once of

King Edward VIII., now H.R.H. The Duke of Windsor.

co-operation among themselves, and with Mr. Ramsay Mac-
Donald, who was our first Labour Prime Minister, at its head,
a National Government was formed, consisting of members
of the Conservative, Liberal and Labour Parties. At a
General Election the whole country approved of that bold
step and gave the new Government an enormous majority,
with the result that conditions soon improved, unemployment
went down and a return to prosperity came.

And then, in May, 1935, when King George was in his
seventieth year, his reign came to its Silver Jubilee ; and in a
celebration of those twenty-five years of great difficulties and
yet of duty greatly done, of dignity and royal devotion to
their interests, the peoples of the Empire united in paying to
him and to his gracious consort, Queen Mary, a tribute of
pride and love.

But early in 1936 our good King again fell ill, and to the
deep grief of his people at home and beyond the seas, at a
few minutes before midnight on the 20th of January, died.

I cannot tell how very sad not only we Britons within the
Empire—" a great Family " he had called us in a Christmas-
day broadcast—were made by the loss ; but every nation of
the world paid to his memory the tributes due to his simplicity
of heart, modesty, wisdom and the high ideals that he had
held and practised. So in pride and honour the noble
King George was borne to his resting-place at Windsor.

He was succeeded by his eldest son, King Edward the
Eighth ; who already in the spirit of fine service, after many
experiences of travel and administration, in times of war and
of peace, had proved himself worthy to reign after the
traditions of his father.

But not for long was he destined to wield the sceptre over
the British Commonwealth of Nations, for less than a year

after his Accession he felt the call of private happiness and repose, and, to the deep regret of his subjects over the seas and in these home-islands, decided to renounce the throne and abdicate. This he did after days of most earnest anxiety —of sorrow and of wonder—to all, to be succeeded by his brother, the Duke of York. On his Accession Prince Albert, as he had been, gratified his subjects by assuming the name to which his father had brought a restored dignity and shining honour and as His Majesty King George the Sixth, with his gracious Consort, Queen Elizabeth, and their daughters, the Princesses Elizabeth and Margaret Rose, we hope and pray that for many years to come he will be spared to rule the Empire in happiness and prosperity.

GOD SAVE THE KING

THE END

INDEX

PRINTED IN GREAT BRITAIN BY WILLIAM CLOWES AND SONS, LIMITED,
LONDON AND BECCLES.